KT-503-571

Nicola Saladino

ATLAS of art

LORENZO the MAGNIFICENT
and the Florentine Renaissance

Traduzione di Kristina Nastopkaitė

DEMETRA

Design, layout and editing: Sedigraf, Blevio (CO)

Photographs: Sedigraf archives

Sedigraf would like to thank all those who have contributed to the iconographic research. Sedigraf is prepared to settle possible claims regarding pictures published for which has not been possible to obtain their source.

ATLAS OF ART
LORENZO THE MAGNIFICENT
AND THE FLORENTINE RENAISSANCE
1ª edizione aprile 2001
© DEMETRA S.r.l.
Via Strà 167 – S.S. 11
37030 Colognola ai Colli (VR)
Tel. 045 6159711 - Fax 045 6159700

Introduction

Florence is the capital of the Italian and European Renaissance and therefore the crossroad of this extraordinary period experienced by western society. Knowing the grandness of Florentine civil, cultural and artistic heritage, it is impossible not to avoid cutting out relevant parts, in this way risking to sacrifice important aspects of this great and complex phenomenon. Therefore this unrepeatable period of human history was looked through selecting priorities with difficulty and sometimes priorities of priorities.

The historical background is analysed in its most important features in order to give the necessary references to social and economical, internal and foreign politics. Many genial intellectuals and artists worked inside this splendid "container" – Florence in the XIV and XV centuries that is to say the Florence of the Medici. Their distinctive characteristics are described analysing their most important works rather than meaninglessly listing all of them. Unfortunately, many artists are just named, but we hope we have managed to describe the general creative and absolutely original cultural environment. The everyday life, the city folklore and traditions have not been neglected also taking into account the poorer classes, which indirectly contributed to the great movement of the Renaissance.

Florence is distinguished from any other city mostly for its artistic enthusiasm. In this field we came across the hardest selection: the attention dedicated to the stylistic features of the three major arts should compensate the omission of some great personalities.

Public entertainment

Florence was surely famous during the Renaissance for its hunting and magnificent banquets, often accompanied by dances, which involved mainly great families' birthday or wedding celebrations. Those events though, were not the only entertainment in the city: many other **feasts** were **public** and equally involved **aristocrats**, **bourgeois** and **common people**.

The most popular event was the *palio*. The race would take place around Florence, from Porta a Prato to Porta Santa Croce and the crowd would fill the streets to support its favourites. The horses and their riders (some years later the horses would race **without jockeys**) carried the badges of the lords, the owners of the animals. The contenders would wait for the starting signal: the tolling of the bell of Torre della Signoria. Finally, some judges, seated on a special grandstand near Porta Santa Croce, would record the order of arrivals. The winner would receive the *palio*, an elegantly embroidered drapery, which was then put on a chariot that would move around the city for the admiration of the audience. Another great amusement was the lions show. The lions were considered to be the symbol of Florence's strength and independence and it was the citizen's duty to feed them. There was a special cage for the lions, near the government palace, which was opened on important occasions to bring the beasts to the main square. Here an artificial forest had been created for the preys to hide (stags or buffaloes). Around this hunting area wooden stands were located for the audience. Obviously, the show was not very safe and sometimes the lions would attack people, causing mortal incidents.

Nowadays Florentine soccer is still followed with great enthusiasm.

Another very famous feast was the Carnival. During the celebration a parade of originally decorated carnival floats, carrying young people dressed up as mythological heroes, would proceed along the streets.

The world-wide known Florentine soccer was already played by the lower classes. During the Renaissance, though, the rules had not been defined yet and soccer was not an institution which involved all the citizens as it would in the later centuries.

Music was very appreciated in Florence, even among the least educated people. In 1480 **ANTONIO SQUAR- CIALUPI**, a famous organist, founded a music school with the support of Lorenzo il Magnifico, in order to spread the knowledge of the most common musical instruments of that time: organ, harpsichord, violin, cello, lyre, harp, lute, horn. The important role of music in the Renaissance culture is also shown in the well-known painting theme of the *sacra conversazione*, typical of contemporary Venetian paintings. In these works the musicians are depicted with a symbolic function: music was considered to be a link between God and mankind. The concerts were usually played by string quartets.

At the beginning of the 16th century a Venetian organist, called **STEFANELLO**, had the genial idea of **accompanying** drama with music in a sort of dialogic development of the action. This invention had great success in Florence and **POLIZIANO** wrote dramas played along with more than one orchestra: every character, in fact, was identified by different musical instruments. In the refrains, then, all the musicians and actors would play and sing the same motif.

Finally, during the Renaissance, the theatre left behind its original religious character, deriving from the schemes of the *sacra rappresentazione*, and became a laic performance: the scenes moved from the churches to the gardens of aristocratic palaces.

Title page of an edition of the Mandragola, *published around thirty years after the first one. We know that the representation of Machiavelli's play had an enormous success among all social classes in Florence.*

Court manners

I n Florence, after **COSIMO DE' MEDICI** had transformed (1434) his power into a sort of dictatorship, his heirs created a proper dynasty. It is easy to imagine how strong the opposition of the democrats to this leadership was such opposition was also supported by the great families. The Medici, and particularly **LORENZO**, though, were good at smothering this discontent, "distracting" the public opinion with many amusements.

Renaissance Florentines were really fond of money. Yet, they were neither greedy nor drunkards: these vices, which they considered typical of the Germans and the British, were not endured in the city. Lorenzo il Magnifico himself was a humble prince in his everyday life, even if he never missed the occasion to organise huge feasts. He would personally take care of the ceremonial and write specific poems to suggest the themes of the celebrations.

The banquets were the most important occasion for socialising in Florence; all nobles and bourgeois had to organise some during the year for their clients and friends. For

A great wedding banquet in a painting by Botticelli.

Lorenzo's wedding with Clarice Orsini, in June 1479, the loggia and the palace gardens hosted five banquets in three days, and more then one hundred calves were slaughtered for the feast! Florentines really cared about the ceremonial and good manners at the table and they would follow the behaviour indicated in many novels of Boccaccio's *Decamerone*. Monsignor **GIOVANNI DELLA CASA** (1503-1556), poet and humanist, kept in mind Boccaccio's teachings while writing his **Galateo** (1551-1554). The title comes from the name of a bishop, Galeazzo ("Galatheus" in Latin) Florimonte, who had suggested the theme. **This treatise on good manners and civil rules for living together would strongly influence western society in later centuries.** The main character of the book is an old man who, even if not educated, is very wise. He teaches his pupil how to dominate natural instincts and consequently keep an elegant and good behaviour, because "possessing good manners is very similar if not equal to a virtue". Monsignor della Casa, then, wrote about those acts or discussions to avoid because they may result inconvenient or displease the senses. He also gave advice on clothing, which should always be coherent with the situation.

Monsignor Giovanni della Casa, in an XVIII century engraving.

There are many colourful examples in the book: he suggests not to scratch or spit while eating, not to eat too fast to avoid embarrassing hick-ups, or not to clean one's teeth with a handkerchief...

It is quite strange to note how toasting was not common yet: the author considered it a very bad habit. On the other hand, excessive drinking was against the supreme ideal of "moderation" that dominated the whole of society. Without it, in fact, "good is not beautiful and beauty is not pleasant".

Finally, in *Galateo*, Florentine pragmatism involves good manners as well and Della Casa underlines the benefits of good behaviour and proper attitude, which "help their *possessors* not less than a great mind".

Banks and Fiorini

P olitics in Florentine economy had a very important mediating role: complicated rules regulated the life of the civil community and the division of the population into corporations. There were 21 corporations: 7 major guilds and 14 minor guilds. The first ones were the guilds of the middle classes, which were in favour of great families; the second ones were the guilds of the common people – their support allowed the Medici's coming to power.

Four main major guilds established the city welfare: **calimala**, **wool**, **silk** and, above all, **banks**. The first, the guild of merchants – whose name derived from *Calis Malus* ("Mala street"), a Florentine street of bad fame – was the most ancient one and had the greatest juridical independence. It was autonomously regulated, because the city government, overwhelmed by inner fights, was not able to guarantee stableness. **The business of the merchants was based mainly on the import** of raw **materials**, mostly from FRANCE, which were then sold to the Florentine industry for finishing operations.

The guild of wool imported raw materials from SPAIN and from BRITAIN. For centuries it had been the leading textile

An Italian banker at work, miniature from De septem vitiis; *late XIV century (London, British Museum).*

industry, until, in the fourteenth century, it went through a crisis due to foreign competition. Soon it was overtaken by the guild of silk, which used the advantage of **technical innovations**. Producing high quality goods, Florentine silk was equal or even superior to the silk of FLANDERS, for long considered the best in Europe.

However, **the** guild **of banks was the main guild for Florentines**. The bankers and the moneychangers of the city would gather in Mercato Nuovo (the New Market) where the exchange rate was more practical and secure due to the discovery of the **bill of exchange**. Florentine **commercial stations**, spreading throughout the whole of Europe, created a vast network. In this way the *fiorini*, being famous for their solidity, would freely travel around the entire continent.

Some Florentine bankers issued huge loans to powerful foreign kings both in favourable as well as risky conditions. Many of them succeeded very quickly; some of them, though, had to face serious problems of bank liquidity. This occurred to two of the three greatest Florentine families – the Bardi and the Peruzzi. In 1345 **they went bankrupt due to the refusal of Naples' and England's kings to pay back their enormous debts**.

The fifteenth century gave rise to a new generation of bankers. All of them were of merchant origin, yet, they were certainly more cautious and, most probably, better organised. The most famous ones were the Datini, the Pazzi and, above all, the Medici. Cosimo de' Medici, who inherited the banking business from his father, Giovanni, was the absolute leader of the internal city market. Moreover he had two branch houses in VENICE, two in ROME, one in NAPLES and took care of the major part of the Pope's financial deals. In a city like Florence, where not to have money was considered degrading, bankers' activities were surely the best way to conquer political power... This worked the other way around as well: **the Medici more than once managed to change the financial politics of the government together with the economical system of the whole of Florence. Such changes would aim to improve the welfare of their own family**.

The golden Fiorino, minted in 1254, popular currency all over Europe.

The *Ville* and their gardens

The XIV century appeared one of the most riotous periods in the history of the Republic of Florence. The city was constantly threatened by inner riots and foreign dangers, which caused the strategic need of defending the countryside with castles as military outposts.

During the XV century, when, due to the principality, Florence regained its social and political stability, the countryside got safer and therefore became landed property. Such process was encouraged by the flow of capital from the urban industrial and commercial economies, in crisis, to the more reassuring agricultural investments. The defensive function of castles was diminishing and they slowly became **places of amusement**, where to organise hunting or to escape from summer heat and plagues, still common at that time. The Medici were one of the first families to encourage this **transformation of castles from military outposts into residences**. Such initiative hid propoganda purposes, that is to say it wanted to demonstrate the economical and social power of the Medici. Such return to the Arcadian nature was also influenced by the readings of Virgilio's **Bucolicon liber** and **Georgicon libri**. Countryside *ville* and gardens were also considered perfect examples of synthesis between natural and artificial beauty; they seemed ideal places for the rediscovered classical **otium**.

In 1434 Cosimo il Vecchio commissioned to **MICHELOZ-ZO** (1396-1472) the construction of the **Villa of Careggi**. The architect, facing a building which had never been treated before by Renaissance architecture, took a conservative choice and simply revised the model of a medieval castle. The walls structure seems very closed (apart from the wing with a portico and a dominating loggia) and a heavy gallery rises

Medici's Villa of Careggi, commissioned by Cosimo il Vecchio to Michelozzo. Lorenzo il Magnifico chose it for the seat of the Platonic Academy.

on suspended arches. Even if the architectural style of the façade is still medieval, its plan reveals a very rational division of space, which is especially characteristic to Renaissance. Worth mentioning is also the garden, decorated with a fountain by **VERROCCHIO**. Lorenzo il

Medici's Villa of Poggio a Caiano, renovated by Giuliano da Sangallo and commissioned by Lorenzo il Magnifico.

Magnifico chose the *Villa* of *Careggi* for the seat of the Platonic Academy. In 1451, after the success of his first villa, Michelozzo was given the responsibility to transform the **Castle of Cafaggiolo** into a residence. Peculiar of this villa are numerous towers, situated in an asymmetric way, which, together with opened spaces in the façade, make the structure dynamic.

Very different is the **Villa of Poggio a Caiano** (1485-1513), which stands as the most famous Renaissance example of this architectural type of building. Originally as property of the Cancellieri family, the building was then owned by the Strozzi and then by the Rucellai, who in 1479 passed it to Lorenzo il Magnifico. The latter instructed **GIULIANO DA SANGALLO** (1445 approx.-1516) to transform the construction into a house worth its glorious owner. The medieval models reintroduced by Michelozzo were not acceptable anymore due to the modern ideas of the commissioner. The architect, therefore, following the example of Giuliano di Maiano, who was a little older found his own model in classical forms, still creating a totally new structure. The construction was situated on a squared platform made of arches. Through two staircases (originally straight but nowadays semi-circular due to a renewal in the seventeenth century) one enters a wide atrium framed by a classical *pronaos*, inserted in the façade – the scheme characteristic to Palladio. Thanks to its harmonic proportions, the building, surrounded by a huge park, had to inspire a sense of great serenity.

The Pretaia, already owned by the Medici family, was enlarged by Bernardo Buontalenti (1531-1608) following the wish of Fernando I.

The *Palazzi*

T he modern definition of *palazzo* (**mansion**) **as a** building type **derives from the Florentine buildings of the Renaissance**. Till the 15th century civil architecture had been developing very unsteadily, since there was a lack of defined forms and strict principles of order, which could have permitted the comparison with sacred architecture, the only one to be the object of high architecture.

Leon Battista Alberti, Palazzo Rucellai, the façade (1450-1460, Florence).

The entirely Florentine "invention" of *Palazzi*, was put into theory by **LEON BATTISTA ALBERTI** in his *De architectura libri decem*. This work established the canons of urban architecture that characterise Italian historical centres also in our days, indicating precise rules of methods and style.

Great Florentine families, such as the Medici, the Riccardi, the Rucellai, the Pitti, who were constantly fighting between themselves, used the *Palazzi* as their fortresses within the city. Not by chance the façade organised in three levels – scanned by floor signing frames, which consisted of *bugnato rustico* (rough stones sticking out from the wall) or *conci* (dressed stones) in its inferior part – reminded the structure of the *castrum* (Roman castle) more symbolically than aesthetically. The outside appearance surely gave the impression of steadiness and solidity yet not making the structure heavy. The impression of lightness was often obtained by several horizontal rows of *lesene* (bas-relief columns) and a vertical succession of the three orders of classical architecture: Tuscanic-Doric, Ionic and Corinthian (going from the massive to the slender). This was shown in the examples of Vitruvian architecture such as the Colosseum, whose structure was very well known in the Renaissance.

The ground floor, logically the most difficult to defend, had the entrance to the palace through huge strengthened doors, impossible to break down. During peaceful times, these doors would also facilitate the commercial activities inside the courtyard, which was surrounded by different levels of porticos. On the same floor enormous cells for food would guarantee a long autonomy in case of siege.

The living part would usually occupy the first or the second floor. In the first palaces it was reachable by a non-monumental staircase which for security reasons was situated at the corners of the courtyard, quite far from the entrance hall. The staircase was illuminated by large decorated windows shaped as the classical *biforas* (mullioned windows), consisting of a central column and an enhancing arch. For obvious reasons, there were no such windows on the ground flour, where the light would mostly

Michelozzo, a view of Palazzo Medici-Riccardi (above) and its courtyard (below).

come from the courtyard and from the slits protected by iron grids facing the street.

The servants used to live in the attic with low ceiling and little thermic insulation. The rooms were illuminated and ventilated by some skylights, hidden from the perspective of the street by large ornate cornices.

Finally, one must add that the *Palazzi* also had a role of public utility within the city: huge arcades would protect the pedestrians from the sunlight and the marble benches under it would offer a rest to the merchants waiting for their turn.

General aspects

Complicated and continuous cultural discussions have been going on about Humanism, Renaissance and their chronological limits. Everyone, though, agrees upon the fact that **Florence was the cradle of one of the most splendid periods of human history**. The two terms – Florence and Renaissance – appear so intimately together that it becomes almost impossible to use one without immediately evoking the other.

After the year one thousand, the success of communes gave new strength to the political, social, cultural and artistic life of the peninsula. This regeneration reached its peak in the XV century and in the first half of the XVI century, with the actual period of Renaissance.

An image of Florence in the XV century, in a print of that time.

At the time of Dante (1265-1321) and even more at the time of Petrarca (1304-1374) and Boccaccio (1313-1375), Florence was already experiencing the conditions of its future "golden age". In fact, the next century, gave birth to many intellectuals, artists and patrons and a unique synergy took place among economics, politics and culture, giving the city its greatest season.

Italy and all Europe would benefit from the influence of the Florentine Renaissance. When, in the XVI century, the slow decline of the Renaissance began, a new conception of life had already spread out in western society, together with an unreachable zest for harmony, beauty and art. Nowadays, a visitor can

The State as a work of art

This title is the key phrase of the first part of the book *Civilisation of the Renaissance in Italy* by the Swiss historian Jacob Burckhardt (1818-1897). It applies to the formation of Italian *signorie* and principalities during the XV and the XVI centuries. The second part of the book analyses the relations that take place (or should take place) between the State and the single individual. The third part brings up the theme of the cultural and social consequences of the revived passion for classical civilisation. The fourth part focuses on the "discovery" of the world and mankind by Renaissance intellectuals and artists, which was due to a deeper knowledge of cosmography and natural sciences on one hand and a greater consciousness of human nature on the other. The forms of social life (the feasts, for example) and, in the end, the relationship between morality-religion and contemporary life are the topics of the two last parts of the book. Even though modern critics might find some inevitable methodological limits in this monumental work by Burckhardt, they should still recognise its integrity. The individualism of the Renaissance, in fact, is the *leitmotiv* of the work and connects the central themes throughout all its parts. In this sense, the main role attributed to Florence in this extraordinary and unrepeatable period seems absolutely justified nowadays too.

still feel the same atmosphere while admiring the monuments of the period or simply walking around the streets of the Tuscan capital.

People were conscious of this process and, for instance, Leon Battista Alberti, in his *De pictura* (1436), noticed how artists such as Brunelleschi, Donatello and Masaccio, even without direct references, had finally given an example of greatness to be imitated. On the other hand, Machiavelli said: "This province seems to be born to raise things from death, as we saw in poetry, painting and sculpture."

Since the end of the Roman Empire none of the Italian cities had such a great history. Jacob Burckhardt, in his fundamental book, *Civilisation of the Renaissance in Italy*, said: **"The most elevated political thought and the most varied forms of human development are found united in the history of Florence, which in this sense deserves the name of the first modern State in the world"**.

Historical background

All Dante's Divine Comedy, *and particularly the Hell, testifies the dramatic division of Florence in factions, during late Middle Ages (in the illustration Dante meets Farinata, a Florentine who was older than the poet and belonged to the opposite party).*

It is difficult, as already mentioned before, to define the period of the Renaissance without receiving any objections from the experts on the subject. However, there is a certain fact in the history of Florence: its inhabitants were aware of living in an extremely creative period, which was drastically different from the past. No one else but the intellectuals of the 15th century adopted the term **media aetas** (Middle Ages) to indicate the period, which separated the splendour of ancient times from the richness of their own period.

In the middle of the 14th century, Florence had already experienced the local fights within the Guelph party, between the Bianchi (the faction close to the Ghibelline party, which represented minor nobility) and the winners Neri (the faction which represented the middle classes). Afterwards, **Florence went through a period of serious economical crisis**. Many were the reasons: the bankruptcy of great bankers such as the Bardi and the Peruzzi, the Black Death of 1348, the bloody wars with MILAN and BOLOGNA. In a situation of many social conflicts, Florence faced strikes in the textile field, which had their climax in 1378 with the **riot of the *Ciompi***, the wool labourers.

In order to end the local conflicts, in 1382, a **Merchants oligarchy**, ruled by the Albizzi family, was established, bringing stableness back to the city. Even though some economical fields still had certain difficulties (the wool market was threatened by foreign competition and the banking activity was diminishing), **in the last years of the 14th century the Florentine economical situation was rapidly recovering**. This recovery was due to several factors, such as the strengthening of the silk market, which soon became as important as the wool market, and the development of the art of dying, which gained a very high quality. The Black

Death had diminished the population (from one hundred thousand to thirty thousand) and in this way the relation between the territory and its population was balanced. Low availability of labour caused not only the increase of salaries but, above all, encouraged the research of more efficient methods of production.

As far as foreign affairs is concerned, Florence stopped the expansion of the Visconti, the lords of Milan, and, in 1406, managed to occupy Pisa, which had always been the enemy.

A medal commemorating the Pazzi's conspiracy (Florence, Museo Nazionale del Bargello).

In 1434 **COSIMO DE' MEDICI** became the ruler of the city, due to the support of the middle classes and the help of Venice, which was looking for a faithful partner against Milan. In the same year the pope inaugurated the church of Santa Maria del Fiore. **FRANCESCO SFORZA**, mercenary captain at that time, expanded and protected the walls of the city. Some years later Francesco, supported by Florence, which wanted to limit the growth of Venice, took the power in Milan. Therefore Venice, which was trapped between the two fronts, allied with Naples and Genoa, so that Italy was shaken by both parts trying to take over. In 1454 Italian states signed the peace of Lodi, which was the great success of Cosimo's politics: the states agreed upon keeping the peace in the peninsula by practising **politics of balance**, in order to protect their territories from the expansion of strong foreign monarchies.

At the same time, though, **fiscal pressure magnified the social differences within Tuscany**. Some families, which had economical activities abroad and therefore did not have to pay taxes, went on getting richer and richer, whereas the major part of the population was under the burden of heavy taxes and was becoming poorer and poorer.

Cosimo kept the power till his death in 1464, but only in 1458 he reorganised the communal structure of the city, changing some laws of the republic and, in this way, gaining an absolute power. When he died, he was recognised as *Pater patriae* (Father of the motherland).

The power was then inherited by his son **PIERO** who was favoured by being very rich and having a governing experience at the side of his father. Weak health conditions, though, brought **PIERO** to a premature death.

The entrance of Carlo VIII, the king of France, in Florence.

In 1469 the power was taken over by Lorenzo, at that time twenty years old. Lorenzo was extremely skilled at gaining the support of the middle classes. This support did not get weaker even when he changed the laws of the republic in order to favour his powerful family. In1478, the famous conspiracy of the Pazzi, a rich Florentine family hostile to the leadership of the Medici, was organised with the approval of the pope. The revolt managed to harm only Lorenzo's brother, **GIULIANO**, and then was immediately stopped by the insurrection of the people. The Pazzi were executed together with those who approved of them, including the cardinal Riaro, whose death caused an excommunication from the pope. This caused a conflict with two different forces taking sides: on one side the **PAPAL STATES** and **NAPLES**; on the other side Florence, **MILAN** and **VENICE**. Lorenzo demonstrated his diplomatic skills and re-established the peace, respecting the principle of balance that was agreed upon twenty years earlier in Lodi.

Due to the obtained success, which further increased Lorenzo's prestige, he could conclude the phase of the republic – which had remained just a formality – and transform the city into a *signoria*, governed together with a Council of seventy faithful members. The conflicts, though, had weakened the economy of Florence. This was also caused by the economical losses of the Medici, although it did not influence negatively the cultural life and the artistic production of that time.

In 1492 **GIOVANNI**, Lorenzo's son, became cardinal, which was another important step in his ecclesiastic career before becoming pope **LEONE X** in 1513. The same year was marked by the death of Lorenzo, at that time already universally known as **IL MAGNIFICO**.

The power was inherited by Lorenzo's son **PIERO** who, not having the political capacities of his father, quickly lost the support of the people. In this way Florence had to pass, without any resistance, its supremacy over central Italy to **CARLO VIII**, king of FRANCE.

FRATE GEROLAMO SAVONAROLA, a passionate predicator determined to purify ecclesiastic and civil politics from the evil of corruption, took advantage of the dissatisfaction of the people. In 1494 **a riot of the masses put an end to the power of the Medici** and Savonarola founded a new republic, opened to the interests of the common people. Savonarola's severe social politics soon caused the hostility of the powerful Florentine families and the pope, who ex-communicated him. The economical crisis contributed to the dissatisfaction also of those who had been supporting the priest and soon the latter was isolated. In 1498 **Savonarola was arrested and condemned to death**.

However, the republic remained and **PIERO SODERINI** ruled the state till 1512. During that year **the Medici re-entered Florence and took the power back**. It was car-dinal **GIOVANNI**, together with his brother **GIULIANO**, who brought the Medici to their old splendour. When Giovan-ni became pope, he left the authority of the city to his nephew **LORENZO**, who would always be in-fluenced by the politics of the pope. In 1527, after various and not very successful heirs, the Medici were exiled and the re-public was re-established.

At the same time in Europe the battle be-tween **FRANCESCO I**, king of France, and **CARLO V**, the emperor, was going on. Flo-rence was supporting the French, while Rome, ruled by pope **CLEMENTE VII**, Gio-vanni de' Medici's cousin, was on the em-peror's side. After years of brave resistance, Florence had to give up in 1530 due to the siege of the emperor. Carlo V wanted to re-ward the support received from Rome by assigning to **ALESSANDRO DE' MEDICI** the government of the Florentine republic and giving him as wife his daughter Margherita. **This is how the princedom of the Medici, which later would become a grand duchy, ruled by COSIMO I, started**.

Savonarola's sharp profile, in a canvas painted by his Dominican brother Bartolomeo della Porta (1475-1517), kept at the Museum of the monastery of San Marco in Florence.

HIERONYMI·FERRARIENSIS·ADEO·
MISSI·PROPHETÆ·EFFIGIES·

Florence and the Medici family

F lorence had always been proud of being a republic and, at the beginning of the XV century, its laws would prevent any attempt to concentrate the political power in one person's hands. Which important events took place that made the Medici family rise so fast in the social hierarchy?

The Medici had come from the valley of Mugello in the north of Florence and settled down in Florence in the first years of the XIII century. In the next century the family got richer, but still did not have any of its members in important political positions. This was probably due also to the internal family conflicts that were ruining its public reputation.

In the middle of the XIV century some Medici started getting involved in politics, supporting the ideas of the common people. The riots of that period caused the exile of many members of the family and even seven branches of the family tree were banned from occupying public roles. The main representative of one of the two branches remaining was **GIOVANNI DI BICCI** (1360-1429), who started the **banking activity**. Soon he gained a good position in the financial affairs of the pope and **made the Medici the richest family in Europe**. In 1402 he was elected for the first time member of the *signoria*: this was his first step towards power. In 1429 "he died very rich in money, but even more in fame and good reputation" (Machiavelli).

Giovanni had given his son Cosimo (see pg. 19) a **classical education** which dignified his wealth and directed him towards **patronage**, an aspect of his civic politics that would make him very popular. Taking advantage of the continuous wars, which were forcing the Florentine government to ask financial support from the richer families, Cosimo progressively gained fame as the richest man in the city. Later many **weddings**

The cloister of the Laurentian Library, founded by Cosimo il Vecchio and enlarged by Lorenzo, later on named after him.

between the Medici and the more ancient
Florentine families, such as the Bardi, the
Salviati and the Cavalcanti, took place. That, together with a system of favouritism, which
would assure protection for political support,
enabled him to ignore the severe laws of the republic and create the basis for a political party.
Such party was aiming to gather many people of
influence that could vote for the Medici in public elections, and was also practising propaganda on the lower classes. The strength of the
Medici's party lay in its union: the opponents
were probably stronger, but were constantly
fighting among themselves.

In 1433 the highest position of the Republic
was given to **BERNARDO GUADAGNI**, a man dominated by the Albizzi, generally known as hostile
to the Medici. **Guadagni was convinced to condemn
Cosimo for attempting on the order of the republic** and
exiled him and other members of his family for ten years.

*Cosimo de' Medici, also
called "il Vecchio" ("The old
man"), in a portrait
by Pontormo (1494-1556),
kept in the Uffizi.*

The next year new elections brought to power the party
in favour of the Medici, which cancelled the penalty and
let Cosimo, warmly welcomed by the nation, return to the
city. From that moment on, the city was in the hands of
**the Medici who became one of the greatest dynasties
in Europe**.

For thirty years Cosimo ruled the destiny of the state,
almost never appearing personally in important positions, but making sure that these would be occupied by
faithful people.

We previously spoke about the splendid foreign politics
of Cosimo (see pg. 11), but one cannot leave out his contribution in the artistic field. Under his patronage the
most prestigious artists and intellectuals of the time started their activities. He founded the Platonic Academy and
sponsored the construction, restoration and completion
of the numerous monuments of the city: the church of
Santa Maria del Fiore, the monastery of San Marco, the
façade of Santa Maria Novella...

Cosimo had two children: **Piero** (1414-1469) and **Giovanni** (1421-1463). The first one, educated by the best human-

Piero de Medici portrayed in a bust by Mino da Fiesole, kept in the Florentine Museum of the Bargello.

ists of the time, ruled the city for some years and followed the patronage policy initiated by his father; the other one dedicated himself to the economic interests of the family.

Piero, called "il Gottoso" ("the Gouty") for his inherited hyperuricaemia, was the father of **Lorenzo** (1449-1492), who became il **Magnifico**. The latter, together with his brother **Giuliano** (1453-1478), inherited the power and kept it in his own hands after the violent death of his brother, during the conspiracy of the Pazzi (as we already saw before). Lorenzo used the sword and diplomacy to re-establish his supremacy and took advantage of the first favourable occasion to transform Florence into a *signoria*. We will speak more in detail about Lorenzo il Magnifico as the symbol and the mind of the Florentine Renaissance later (see pg. 26-29).

Lorenzo had three male children: **Piero** (1472-1503), **Giovanni** (1475-1521) and **Giuliano** (1478-1516). The first one took the power from his father with dramatic political consequences, having to face the hostility even of the common people, who were the main support of the Medici in the city. Therefore he was exiled with all his family in 1494: this was the period of Savonarola's republic (see pg. 21). Giovanni, named cardinal in 1492 by pope Innocenzo VIII, became pope in 1513, named **Leone X**. He managed to re-establish the power of his family in the city, which he ruled for some years together with his brother Giuliano.

The governing was then taken over by **Lorenzo** (1492-1519), later named **duke of Urbino**, nephew of Giovanni, who tried to follow the magnificent traces of his homonymous predecessor. However, constantly under high pressure from the pope, he never managed to establish solid politics nor to obtain the support of the masses, even though he had a good reputation among intellectuals such as **Machiavelli** who dedicated to him his work *Il principe*.

After Lorenzo's death, the state was briefly ruled by **Giulio** (1478-1534), Giovanni's cousin. When named pope **Clemente VII**, he had to leave the power to cardinal **Silvio Passerini** as a temporary regent of the young **Ippolito** and **Alessandro** de' Medici.

The situation of the Medici family was not the same as in the old times: **the dissatisfaction of the common people was growing and strong political figures**, which would be able to gain the support of the masses, **were missing**. There were numerous attempts to re-establish the republic: in 1527 the republican riots had their peak and **the Medici were forced to leave the city again.**

The exile was not long because in 1531 **Carlo V** assigned the Florentine government to **Alessandro** de' Medici (1512-1537), husband of his daughter **Margherita** and therefore prince. Alessandro de' Medici by many contemporary intellectuals was considered *a corrupted and immoral person* although his politics was strongly supported by the bright intellectual **Guicciardini** (1483-1540).

Clemente VII (in the picture) was Leone X's cousin. Due to his politically ambiguous behaviour, he suffered the "sack of Rome" (6th of may 1527) by the storm troops of the emperor Carlo V, whose support, though, was crucial for the election of Cosimo I.

During the Epiphany of 1537, Alessandro was murdered in a conspiracy organised by his cousin Lorenzino, who was aiming for the republic.

Following Guicciardini's advice, Carlo V named **Cosimo I** (1519-1574), son of **GIOVANNI DALLE BANDE NERE**, ruler of Florence. **Cosimo I practised politics of terror and stopped all the attempts of opposition with the sword**. In order to finance the luxury of his splendid court and his ambitious expansionistic politics – which enabled him to conquer SIENA – he oppressed the Florentine nation with **high taxes**. In 1569 Pio V named Cosimo I grand duke of Tuscany.

Since then the Medici would rule the region of Tuscany until 1737, but their state could never again reach the splendour of the Florence in the Renaissance.

Lorenzo: great poet and patron

Lorenzo de' Medici marches among some knights, in a fresco by Benozzo Gozzoli (1420-1497). The balance of forces and the elegance of the painting create an ideal image that corresponds to the one Lorenzo was wishing for.

Lorenzo de' Medici, called il Magnifico, has already been mentioned many times. This has its good reasons: he was indeed the greatest representative of the dynasty of rulers that dominated Italy and made the unique dream of the Renaissance come true.

After a youth dedicated to the studies that were considered crucial for the education of a young prince (he went through **military training** and had his first experience in **diplomacy**), Lorenzo followed the lessons of **poetics** and **oratory** led by **CRISTOFORO LANDINO**, studied **philosophy** and **Greek** with **ARGIROPULO** and often frequented the Platonic Academy of **MARSILIO FICINO**, since the first years of its foundation (1462).

If Cosimo was still a bourgeois and a businessman, Lorenzo was already an aristocrat and his palace had become a real court. Great politician and sensitive towards cultural issues, il Magnifico took very much into consideration the role of intellectuals in the period historically defined as "civil humanism". Lorenzo strongly encouraged all artistic manifestations within the city and even in this field appeared to be an **excellent organiser** and a sensitive **patron** (for all the numerous works commissioned or sponsored by him one should look in the specific chapters on the greatest Florentine artists of that time).

Within Lorenzo's artistic coterie **ANGELO POILIZIANO** and **LUIGI PULCI** had their privileged importance. One following the elitist neo-platonic theories and the other concentrating on brightly populist poetry, they were certainly the closest to the ideas of il Magnifico, together contributing to his **search for equilibrium**.

Lorenzo came to power very young and soon had to face the pressure of neighbouring states and the hostility of powerful Florentine families. Therefore he started an intense diplomatic activity that would bring him to ally with the king of Naples Fernando d'Aragona, to whom he donated the *Raccolta Aragonese*, an anthology of vulgar tongue Tuscan poets introduced by a letter written by Poliziano.

After the conspiracy of the Pazzi (see pg. 20), Lorenzo used diplomacy in order to stop the hostility of foreign countries, primarily the Papal States, and became the balance in Italian political equilibrium.

Giuliano de' Medici, portrayed by Botticelli in the same year of the Pazzi's conspiracy (1478), in which he died. In 1475 Poliziano had started to compose a mythological poem dedicated to Giuliano to celebrate his triumph in a tournament, but the poem was left unfinished because of the tragic and unexpected event (see pg. 34).

In 1484 Lorenzo hosted in Florence **GIOVANNI PICO DELLA MIRANDOLA**, protecting him even when his heterodox ideas caused the anger of the Church. With the help of Pico and Poliziano, Lorenzo **reinforced the Laurentian Library**, which soon became one of the major centres of manuscripts in the peninsula.

As far as literature is concerned, il Magnifico demonstrated a **systematic interest for the vulgar tongue**, so that none of his numerous works were written in Latin.

It is very hard to deduce precisely when his works were written, even more because some of them have not been attributed to him (this is the case, for example, of the *Nencia da Barberino*, in some critics' opinion written by **GIAMBULLARI**). However it is possible to divide his creation into two periods: the **juvenile period** till 1484 and the **mature period**.

In his earlier works one can find neo-platonic traces together with motives derived from popular traditions.

Among them there are some poems such as the famous eclogue of the *Nencia da Barberino*, in which a farmer, in love with a peasant named Nencia, tries to conquer her celebrating her physical virtues with very realistic images. In the short bucolic poem *Altercazione* countryside life is compared to the urban one, coming to the conclusion that real happiness exists only in heaven. Instead, the comical short poem written in octave *Uccelagione di starne* also known as *Caccia al falcone* influenced by Pulci describes a day of hunting in the Florentine countryside which ends with strange and funny adventures. In the *Simposio*, a short burlesque poem also called *Beoni*, a group of Florentine funsters of all social classes who go to a tavern is described in a grotesque key. The last works of this period are the religious poems such as the *Capitoli* and the *Laudi*; the major part of the *Canzoni a ballo*; two novels of Boccacio's type and, in the end, the poems of the *Canzoniere*, inspired by Petrarca (a collection of

Lorenzo il Magnifico surrounded by the most renowned members of his "coterie" (among the others, the humanists Pico della Mirandola and Marsilio Ficino), in a fresco by Vasari.

about one hundred love sonnets mostly dedicated to Lucrezia Donati, in which a **platonic conception of love** appears).

Amongst mature works one finds the major part of the sonnets, of *stil novo* characteristics, together with a series of short philosophical stories (as in Dante's *Vita nuova*), gathered in the anthology *Commento ad alcuni sonetti d'amore* that represents a revival of the *stil novo* in the neo-platonic cultural environment. In the proem of this work il Magnifico touches upon the themes of the already mentioned letter by Poliziano (see pg. 34) and **promotes the vulgar tongue as a language suitable to treat any kind of theme**, as already proved by Dante and Alberti. The growing use of the vulgar tongue had also a political meaning. It helped to increase the prestige of Florence: the city that in the previous century had nourished the greatest writers with this expressive instrument.

In the rest of the poems the themes of *stil novo* dominate; in surely descriptive short poems, such as *Corinto* and *Ambra*, the apparently idyllic tone slowly becomes more and more realistic and the gradual detachment from abstract philosophical conceptions appears evident; the two series of love *strambotti* like *Selve d'amore* are strongly influenced by Poliziano, who was, in that period, devoted to the classical *silvae* (collections of poems with different metre and themes).

Engraving for the Canti carnascialeschi, *composed for the Carnival in 1490 by Lorenzo, who was also the inventor of the allegoric chariots, nowadays still very common.*

Lorenzo's vast literary creation is concluded by the *Rappresentazione di San Giovanni e Paolo*, played in public in 1491, and some *Canti carnascialeschi* for the Carnival of 1490, which were inspired by hedonistic and elegiac morals. In the most famous work of il Magnifico, *Trionfo di Bacco e Arianna*, youth, inevitably destined to fade with time, is celebrated ("Quant'è bella giovinezza / che si fugge tuttavia! / Chi vuol esser lieto sia: / di doman non c'è certezza").

Humanism

The Città ideale ("*Ideal city*"): *the anonymous artist (late XV century) organised the space following the humanistic ideal of "human measure".*

The term "humanism" refers to a cultural movement, which started at the end of the XIV century and which conceived man as the canon of everything, coming back to the positions already expressed by the classical tradition. **The renewed interest for classical authors was not concentrating on religious pre-Christian elements**, as in the Middle Ages, **but was whishing to revive a sensitiveness entirely connected with the terrestrial experience**. The new approach flourished also in philological and historical fields.

The revival of the dignity of values, such as culture and arts, led to a new interpretation of religion: some intellectuals were ignoring it, some others even denied its base, judging it for not completing the needs of contemporary mankind. Humanists generally interpreted Christian religious commitments in the perspective of **civic morality**, which glorifies the merits of virtuous people during their lives. **Mankind becomes fully responsible for its destiny**, being able to dominate the world.

One of the greatest intellectuals involved in such re-interpretation of Christianity was **MARSILIO FICINO** (1433-1499), who, helped by the Medici, founded the Platonic Academy. The aim of the school was to harmonize religious rules with the principles of classical philosophy and firstly platonic. Ficino's pupil **GIOVANNI PICO DELLA MIRANDOLA** (1463-1494) went even further elaborating the theory of **syncretism**, according to which the divine is the synthesis of the truths of all historical religions.

The centres of culture were changing: they were not the universities any longer, but the **academies** and the **courts** of the great dynasties, first of all the Medici in Florence. The popular phenomenon of patronage should not be interpreted as modern propaganda to improve the image and reputation of a ruler, but as a real search for cultural renovation.

Humanists denied the possibility of reaching an absolute united culture, as claimed by theology, and focused on the necessity of an **organic and harmonic development of knowledge** in all its fields: from history to art, from philosophy to mathematical sciences. Humanists celebrated the superiority of one's personal capacities to the collective ones, which were instead glorified in the Middle Ages.

LEONARDO DA VINCI (1452-1519) spread the scientific spirit, based on induction more than on deduction. Great interest therefore was addressed to the **mechanical arts**, which had always been considered minor arts, where direct experience had an essential role. Leonardo himself would claim: "…those sciences that do not come from experience, the mother of any certainty, and do not end with proved phenomena seem to me vain and full of mistakes…". In this period some revolutionary machinery, which changed the life style of many social classes, were invented: for example, the coming of new firearms, which would strongly reduce the role of chivalry.

Anyway, the most revolutionary invention was the movable-type printing, invented by the German **JOHANN GUTENBERG** and the Dutch **LAURENS COSTER** around mid 15th century. This typographic technique allowed a cheaper production of books and therefore favoured a greater diffusion especially among the middle classes, which until then were excluded from the cultural market. With the circulation of social and political books a solid **public opinion**, which would strongly influence socio-political events of that time, developed. Florentine libraries would soon become very important centres of European culture.

The humanists Marsilio da Ficino, Cristoforo Landino, Agnolo Poliziano and Gentile de' Becchi in a fresco by Ghirlandaio.

Literature

In the XV century in Florence the **literary production found its ideal basis in the anthropocentrism**. Intellectuals particularly focused their attention on **the condition and the problems of mankind in its historical concreteness and in its terrestrial dimension**. Thus humanistic works were mostly of the treatise type. This literary genre was strongly renewed, becoming more free and open, even though it would often be written in Latin. No longer regulated by rigid and pre-established medieval schemes, it was suitable to reflect upon the civil and social life (Matteo Palmieri, Leon Battista Alberti), to celebrate active life (Coluccio Salutati) and to meditate on the privileged position of mankind in the universe (Marsilio Ficino). Treatise writers would convince the readers with the strength and clarity of their thoughts; very frequent classical quotations would support their thesis or would function as "bridges" towards very original cultural positions.

A very common literary typology was the **dialogic treatise**, also of classical inspiration, which has to be associated with the diffusion of coteries and academies. The dialogue allowed to reach a conclusion, which would not be a dogmatic claim, but the result of a comparison of different ideas and opinions.

The development of the humanistic culture also changed the epistolary type as well: the humanistic epistle was not just a means of communication any longer, but became a **linguistic "laboratory"** and a field to test more difficult texts. The epistle was then used to express, even in strong and polemical tones, different cultural positions, and therefore became a useful instrument of confrontation.

Initially Latin was the only language; later works in vulgar tongue had a greater agility of style and were free from schemes. Florentine vulgar tongue was already gaining the function of interregional language for cultured people, who would have used Latin before. This conversion in literary treatises from Latin to vulgar tongue was strongly influenced by Leon Battista Alberti in his *De familia* and *De pictura*.

If in the Renaissance ideas and cultural values were mostly expressed by prose, poetry reduced its own thematic fields and its creative function. The lyric works were very numerous, but rarely original, which is to say that there were many poets, but no great poet, so that Benedetto Croce defined the XV century as "the century without poetry".

In the complicated frame of the Renaissance lyric one can still notice a common factor: more consumer forms were dominating. In particular the genre of the **poetry of occasion** that had great success with court audiences. This poetic composition, written for a great event or to celebrate an important person, was based not on aesthetic values or on the inventive effort of the author, but on the research of stylistic skills and sharp-witted speech.

Other literary genres that became popular in the second half of the XV century in Florence and later rapidly spread out in all major cultural centres of Italy were **bucolic poetry** and **rusticale poetry**, situated in the mythical Arcadian and pastoral world. Lorenzo and the intellectuals of his group liked this fine genre full of quotations from classical literature, finding in it clear and familiar

On the other page, marble slab with the Grammar sculpted by Luca della Robbia (1400-1482) for the bell tower of the Florentine cathedral and kept in the Museum of Opera del duomo.

Lorenzo il Magnifico's first son, Piero de' Medici, with Poliziano, who was his tutor following Lorenzo's wish (Ghirlandaio, Sassetti Chapel in Santa Trinità, Florence).

references to contemporary characters and court situations.

Among the most famous Florentine poets one has to mention Agnolo Ambrogini (Montepulciano 1454-Firenze 1494), also called **IL POLIZIANO** after the name of his place of birth (*Mons Politianus*). In 1472 he was already in the group of intellectuals close to Lorenzo il Magnifico, who always appreciated his abilities, awarding him with protection and money. In 1475 Lorenzo assigned him the education of his eldest son Piero. After the conspiracy of the Pazzi in 1478, Poliziano moved with the Medici to the Villa of Cafaggiolo, but soon strong disagreement took place and he left Florence. He stayed at the courts of RAVENNA, VENEZIA, MANTOVA, where he met great humanists. In 1480 Poliziano asked Lorenzo permission to re-enter Florence and the old patron immediately agreed. Since then he never left his city and his famous friend. Poliziano spent his last years studying philology, writing and teaching.

His works were very numerous, in Latin as in vulgar tongue, but his masterpiece is a short poem in octave called *Stanze*, which celebrates the victory of Giuliano de' Medici in a tournament. Although its starting point is surely an epical situation (the writing of the poem was interrupted after the conspiracy of the Pazzi killed Giuliano), the poem does not have the structure of an epical narration and consists of a series of short scenes joined together by a weak conceptual link. The main quality of this work is the author's ability of creating short but very detailed images, with an elegant and musical style, which links Poliziano to the fine sensitivity of Hellenistic poetry.

Typical of Florentine literature in the XV century was the genre of the **metrical romance**, which re-elaborated the long and continuous tradition of **epic ballads**. The narrated stories were the same, but the completely new aspect was the use of irony and comicality, as in the famous *Morgante*, Pulci's masterpiece.

The life of **LUIGI PULCI** (Florence 1432-Venezia 1484) was marked by many difficulties, first of all, the bankruptcy of his family. However, thanks to his literary talent, it did not prevent him from a privileged relationship with the Medici. Since 1461 he became Lorenzo's friend, being appreciated as a **popular poet**. Lorenzo's mother Lucrezia Tornabuoni asked Pulci to write a poem inspired by Carolingian topics, the future *Morgante*.

In 1474 his relationship with the Medici family started to deteriorate so that two years later Pulci polemically decided to interrupt it. Afterwards he worked for the Florentine captain Sanseverino, for whom he took part in many missions, the last one in Venice, where he died.

The *Morgante* was inspired by a Florentine XV century epic ballad to which Pulci added some invented parts. The author was not concerned about the narrative structure and therefore the poem does not have an organic development of the events. Also the psychology and the behaviour of the characters are very stereotype and firm from the beginning to the end. Linguistically, instead, Pulci invented a **new expressiveness**: the comical-playful tradition is developed and renovated through an accurate lexical research. The language itself presents the **hero-comical key** and the **strength of the parody**, which represent the most interesting aspect of the inspiration in this original metric romance.

In a detail of the Resurrezione del figlio di Teofilo e San Pietro in cattedra, *by Filippino Lippo, one can notice the figure of Luigi Pulci, the author of* Morgante: *he is the first one on the left.*

Political writers

After Lorenzo il Magnifico's death, **Florence lost its cultural and artistic hegemony** which passed on to ROME. In these years, though, two great Florentine writers such as Machiavelli and Guicciardini were born. They made a deeper and original criticism of politics and history, which was culturally very significant as a result of the weakness of their city.

NICCOLO' MACHIAVELLI (Florence, 1469-1527) was secretary of the second chancellery in the Florentine republic for a long time. The numerous **diplomatic missions** he was involved in between 1498 and 1512 – for which he also wrote very detailed reports – gave him the opportunity to study from the inside the problems linked to the functioning of a state.

Portrait of Niccolò Machiavelli, attributed to Rosso Fiorentino (1494-1540).

After the end of the republic (1512) and the return of the Medici, Machiavelli went to his lands of Sant'Andrea in Percussina and worked there on his main book: *De principatibus* also known as *Il principe* (1513), **the first modern treatise on political sciences**. Between 1519 and 1520, he wrote the *Discorsi sopra la prima decade di Tito Livio* and the *Dell'arte della guerra*. In 1521 he was named **Florence's official history writer**. In 1527, when a riot expelled the Medici from the city and the republic was declared, Machiavelli in vain hoped to be named secretary. The pain for this unexpected offence brought him to an early death, which left his family in poverty.

In his political works Machiavelli started mostly from Roman examples in order to analyse the difficult historical period of that time, in which **Italian states were threatened by great "barbarian" countries**. He found the causes of the crisis in the **limited dimension**, **civil disorder** and **decline** of Italian states, and even

more in **the lack of a strong power**. If it is true that Machiavelli did not trust the masses, it is also true that he could not find a ruler, among all the corrupted ones, who would be able to exert the power, seen as "the art of governing". For this reason **he was hoping for the coming of a prince who could re-launch Italy** and thought he had found one when he got to know Cesare Borgia, the son of pope Alessandro VI.

However Machiavelli was looking for rules of behaviour derived from the "effectual reality" of things and examined the "virtues" of a prince from the perspective of practical utility and efficiency, leaving moral values apart: "Upon this a question arises: whether it be better to be loved than feared or feared than loved? It may be answered that one should wish to be both, but, because it is difficult to unite them in one person, it is much safer to be feared than loved, when, one must chose between the two". In this attitude of his, for which he was often accused of being cynical, Machiavelli reflected the new Renaissance conception of **a person wholly interested in terrestrial affairs and owner of his own destiny**, against "fortune, who shows her power where valour is not prepared to resist her".

Also **FRANCESCO GUICCIARDINI** (Florence 1483-Arcetri 1540) had numerous **diplomatic experiences**, working for the Medici, the pope and other princes. Starting from Machiavelli's texts, which he carefully analysed in the *Considerazioni sui discorsi del Machiavelli* (1528), Guicciardini found the basis of his political ideas in the **objective observation of facts**. Differently from Machiavelli, in his works (among the others the *Ricordi politici e civili* and the *Storia d'Italia*) **he expressed disillusion towards mankind, unable to dominate the events and "fortune"**, which "is very powerful in human things". This fatalist attitude probably derived from the observation of the political weakness of Italian states.

Guicciardini was also convinced that political phenomena do not have a general ruling principle and therefore systematic projects would be useless. **In fact, he believed it was necessary in history an analysis of the "particular", unique and unrepeatable**.

Great critic Francesco De Sanctis (1817-1883) about Guicciardini

"Guicciardini represents an already resigned generation. He does not have any illusions. And since he does not see any remedy to that corruption, he takes part in it and makes it become his wisdom and his halo. Guicciardini's *Ricordi* is the Italian corruption dignified and codified as a model of life..."

The artistis: humanists and scientists

In the 15th century the interest of society in art and mostly in the beauty of manufactures was increasing, following a new critical consciousness, which also brought to the foundation of a group of laic patrons, private citizens and aristocrats. Moreover, the artists became conscious of the value and the cultural dignity of their work.

Humanistic culture essentially contributed to this evolution of thoughts. In fact, the critical capacity of appreciating beauty, even when it is artificial (which is to say created by a person), was considered one of those qualities that are crucial for an ideal "global" education, typical of humanistic pedagogy. On the other hand, the artists took part with their works in the re-discovery of the ancient and in a **cultural renovation** that made them feel the need of a professional preparation, which would go beyond simple technical knowledge. Interpreting once again **VITRUVIO**, the great classical master, and his masterpiece *De Architectura*, strongly contributed to create a model of the artist as a "literate, drawer, geometer", a person who "would know history, philosophy, music, astronomy, astrology, and have some knowledge of medicine and law".

Many intellectuals of that time united the artistic and writing experience: one should think about the architect **LEON BATTISTA ALBERTI** (1404-1472) and his books *De re aedificatoria*, or about the sculptor and architect **LORENZO GHIBERTI** (1378-1455), the author of the *Commentarii*. Despite their important artistic analysis, the two

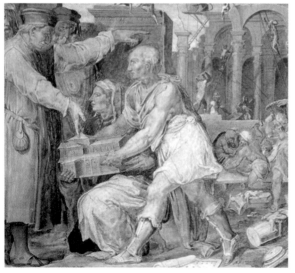

Filippo Brunelleschi presents his model of the new church of San Lorenzo to Cosimo il Vecchio (Giorgio Vasari and assistants, Florence, Palazzo Vecchio).

works were crucial for the diffusion of the new role of the artist: the first one underlined the **theoretical role of the architect**, as already put into practise by Brunelleschi; the second one founded the **theoretical and scientific base for the artistic work**.

Scientific research applied to design was by no doubts a stimulus to enlarge the cultural perspectives of society and contributed to the prestige of the artists. From medieval art, which was focused on symbolic representation of the supernatural reality, the tendencies move towards an art that investigated reality through the **rules which give order to nature**. Starting from these ideas one can understand the new interest for **perspective** (see pg. 43), the **study of proportions**, the research for the best viewpoint in order to create a certain effect, etc.: the artist had to be necessarily an expert in geometry, optics, algebra…

A project of hoist from Leonardo's Codice Atlantico.

If the major part of Florentine artist in the 15th century was still connected to the workshops and economically dependant on patronage, it is also true that among the bourgeois a new tendency towards individualism took place. In the context of the discovery of classical values, this brought to a **revaluation of the strength of individual creative action** and to the full recognition of craft-artistic activity.

When the aristocrats, bankers and merchants wanted to build their palaces and ornate them with paintings and sculptures, in order to make their power tangible and to elevate themselves in the social hierarchy, they felt very close to the ideas of Renaissance artists, who therefore were active participants of the project.

Architecture

As far as the Renaissance artistic revolution is concerned, architecture had a role of major importance, since during this extraordinary historical period it was the branch of learning that contributed the most to the theoretical and practical development of the aesthetic ideal. Two crucial elements of Renaissance art such as **perspective** and the **interest in the ancient** were, in fact, strongly connected to architecture.

Perspective was invented as an instrument for a new subject that was based on the concept of **human space**. Florentine architects were the first to understand the importance of structuring space according to precise geometrical rules that could develop a sense of measure and harmony. People would not be intimidated by the hugeness of gothic buildings; instead they would feel a part of the architectural structure, since mankind was the canon of beauty and the instrument for any comparison.

The façade of the Pazzi Chapel in Florence, in the cloister of Santa Croce, realised according to Brunelleschi's project.

The Renaissance favoured as well a different methodological approach. Architecture changed from empiric (in which the architect was also a technician and therefore had to deal with the construction of his work, which was constantly demanding to change the original plan) to theoretical architecture, in which **the roles of the architect and the technician were separated** and the attention was focused more on the project than on the construction. The use of the project allowed the architects to verify the functional character of a building through complex mathematical rules and to correct eventual structural problems before its construc-

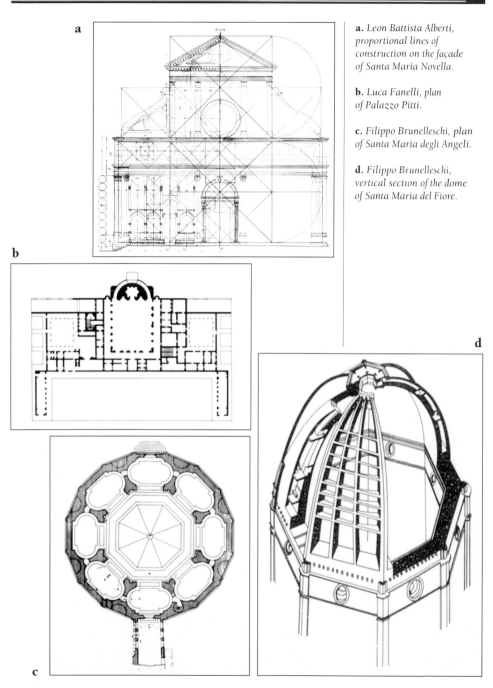

a. Leon Battista Alberti, proportional lines of construction on the façade of Santa Maria Novella.

b. Luca Fanelli, plan of Palazzo Pitti.

c. Filippo Brunelleschi, plan of Santa Maria degli Angeli.

d. Filippo Brunelleschi, vertical section of the dome of Santa Maria del Fiore.

The "bookshop" of the convent of San Marco in Florence, realised by the architect and sculptor Michelozzo Michelozzi (1396-1472), pupil of Brunelleschi, Ghiberti and Donatello.

On the other page, Masaccio's Trinità, *in the church of Santa Maria Novella. Some critics think of a contribution of Brunelleschi to the planning of the perspective background of the fresco.*

tions was begun. Moreover, it allowed the architects to assign the realisation of their projects to someone else: Florentine buildings of that period finished after the death of their creators were not few; one should think about Palazzo Pitti, which many critics attribute to Brunelleschi even though it was built many years after his death.

As far as the "renewed" interest for the ancient is concerned, one may think that the term *Renaissance* means that in this historical period lay the base for the discovery of classical tradition. This conviction is wrong because, actually, during all the Middle Ages classical tradition had never been lost. Most probably it was just "polluted" by different cultural contributions from the nations that were alien to such tradition and from a new Christian perception of the world. During the Renaissance a **new interpretation of classical art** was developed. The new attitude did not bring an imitation of past models, but to a recovery of the theoretical laws that rule the proportions of the elements in ancient buildings, which were admired mostly for their harmony. A new interpretation of such laws had to take into consideration modern technical discoveries, which were the perspective rules. On the other hand the discovery, in 1415, of the book *De Architectura* by the great classical architect Vitruvio surely represented a very important basis to study Greek and Roman canons.

Renaissance architecture found in **central plan buildings** the greatest expression of classical ideals, the perfect metaphor of perfection. This kind of building was, in fact, considered the greatest synthesis of that order and harmo-

The invention of perspective

In technical terms, perspective is a set of rules, which allows to represent a three-dimensional object on two-dimensional surfaces in a way that the image represented corresponds with the one which is seen directly.

The invention of perspective is usually ascribed to Brunelleschi, whereas its theorisation occurs in the treatise *De pictura* written in 1436 by Leon Battista Alberti. The legend says that Brunelleschi had made a painting following the perspective laws in such an accurate manner, that the spectator, forced to observe the image through a hole, could no larger distinguish the real vision from the artificial one, created by the artist.

Perspective had its roots in the principles of medieval optics, which was based on the studies of mirrors and Euclidean geometry. Therefore perspective rules had a feature of duality, which attracted the creativity of the artists: on one hand, since they were based on exact geometrical processes, they were objective; on the other hand, since they were the reproduction of human perception, they were subjective.

Alberti formulated the idea of painting as a window, which looks onto an artificial reality: due to the possibility of eliminating all irrelevant or contradictory elements, perspective space would then become ideal space. Such perspective representation became the main goal of the creative activity of some contemporary artists. Artists such as Leonardo da Vinci brought perspective experimentation to its extremes: their studies on the chromatic variations of an object depending on its distance, led to the invention of the famous aerial perspective.

ny, already mentioned which come out from an ordered and proportioned system of symmetries.

Many central plan buildings were created: first of all the church of Santa Maria degli Angeli, designed by Brunelleschi around 1435 and unfortunately never finished.

Alberti

Apart from architecture Alberti was interested in painting and sculpture, writing two books on these subjects, whose title page is reproduced in this Parisian united edition without date. Also these works testify the theoretical rigour of humanistic spirit, so characteristic to the artistic Florentine environment of the 15th century.

B orn in GENOA in 1404 in a family exiled due to political reasons, died in Rome in 1472, **LEON BATTISTA ALBERTI** studied in the prestigious universities of PADOVA and BOLOGNA, becoming a **typical eclectic humanist**, very cultured, yet without any specific professional education.

He was interested in the arts and mostly in architecture, which more than the others was suitable to scientific research methods.

Differently from Brunelleschi, who, as we will see in further pages, focused his attention on constructive matters, Alberti was passionately concerned with the **stylistic principles that regulate architectural orders**, which he examined with **philological interest**. He contributed in a crucial way to the creation of Renaissance aesthetic ideal, which was based on the search for forms, harmonic and proportioned to human canons. Beauty, in fact, is "the harmony among all members, in the unity to which they belong".

In the first treatise by Alberti, the *De re aedificatoria*, his cultural approach becomes clear: architecture was not considered a practical discipline any longer, but an **intellectual art**, which had to be practised in books and not in building yards. In this way the figure of the architect and the figure of the master builder were distinguished: the first one had to take care of the designing part, the second had to take care exclusively of the realization of the project. Not by chance Alberti always assigned the realization of his buildings to someone else.

Alberti read Vitruvio and rewrote his version of the *De Architectura libri decem*, commenting upon it and ordering in a more organic way the book of the great Roman architect. Alberti, like Vitruvio, believed in the three qualities of architecture: **Utilitas** (utility), **Firmitas** (solidity), **Vetustas** (beauty), but, for the success of a building, he added other three "ingredients": **Numerus** (the number), **Finitio** (proportion), **Collocatio** (collocation).

Alberti studied in detail the five architectural orders (Doric, Ionic, Corinthian, Tuscanic and Composite) and put into theory the **use of the column as the primary decorative element**. Amongst other things he established the use of pillars under the arches and the use of columns under the architrave that gave the base for contemporary reticular structures and perforated walls.

He was the first great town-planner, not just studying the relations between a building and its surroundings, but establishing different functional areas within the city.

Alberti created few buildings, which had great importance in the history of architecture and in later centuries were ideal canons to follow as, for instance, the Malatesta Temple in Rimini.

In FLORENCE, where Alberti lived since 1428, his most important works were the circular tribune in the church of Santissima Annunziata; Palazzo Ruccellai (1446-1470), in which, for the first time in a civil building, he used the system of pillars typical of public Roman architecture (see pg. 14); the small temple of San Sepolcro for the Ruccellai Chapel in San Pancrazio (1467) and the façade of the church of Santa Maria Novella (1456), for which he used the polychrome Florentine marble. This last work, inspired by Roman buildings, is characterized by a pure and linear innovative design and by some original technical solutions, as the two columns that frame and simultaneously amplify the great entrance arch and the great volutes that connect the inferior and the superior orders, a recurring motif of later architecture.

The façade of Santa Maria Novella, which Alberti was asked to complete in 1458.

Brunelleschi

S on of a rich notary, **FILIPPO BRUNELLESCHI** was born in 1377 in Florence, where he died in 1446. He started his artistic studies in the goldsmith's and sculptural field, gaining a **craftsman's education**, very far away from Alberti's humanistic and literary studies. Antiquity, which would become such a passion to encourage numerous trips to Rome since 1402, was, for him, a discovery.

His first important works in sculpture were the two busts of the *Profeti* for the altar of San Jacopo in PISTOIA. Brunelleschi, though, became famous during the contest for the second bronze door of the Florentine Baptistery (1401): his slab with the ***Sacrificio d'Isacco*** ("Isaac's Sacrifice") was very appreciated for its great technical skills, but even more for its revolutionary compositional scheme. Brunelleschi won *ex æquo* with Ghilberti, but refused his prize most probably not to share the commission.

At this point the artist focused his interests on architecture (just after 1420 he would come back to sculpture with the wooden *Crocifisso* ("Crucifixion") for the Gondi Chapel in Santa Maria Novella and the bas-relief medals of the *Evangelisti* ("Evangelists") in the Pazzi Chapel). After the contest, Brunelleschi **went to Rome many times**, also with Donatello, in order to study the sculptures and ruins of classical buildings, which immediately fascinated him for their innovative schemes and constructive techniques, more than for the stylistic aspects, which were highly appreciated by the artists of that time. In 1418 Brunelleschi started his real architectural career, winning a contest for the construction of the dome of the Florentine cathedral organised by the powerful guild of wool, in which Ghiberti took part once again.

The project of Santa Maria del Fiore (Florentine cathedral) – designed by Arnolfo di Cambio (1245-1310 approx.) in 1296 and modified many times by different groups of architects that, after him, took

The dome of Santa Maria del Fiore.

care of the organisation of construction works – originally planned an octagonal intersection between the nave and the transept, covered by a huge dome, which would open in three apses. The problem lay in building a dome that had a diameter of 50 meters (dimensions reached only by the church of Hagia Sophia in Constantinople and by the Pantheon) over a drum made of thin walls, which was at a height of 55 meters. The traditional solution, which suggested using wooden centring, would have been incredibly expensive and even if theoretically it was possible to find beams of this length, there were no craftsmen skilled for this kind of constructive technique, very typical to Gothic cathedrals.

The Ospedale degli Innocenti.

The dome, constructed by Brunelleschi between 1420 and 1436 was a **miracle of civil engineering** and attracted the attention of the world. Brunelleschi used the constructive technique seen in the Pantheon in Rome with a superimposition of horizontal self-supporting layers, which eliminated the problem of the centring, and used a pointed shape rather than the hemispheric one in order to diminish the lateral pressure of the arches. He also used a double shell structure externally supported by eight angular flying ribs and by sixteen internal ribs, fortifying the structure even more with the use of tie beams, rings of stone and herring-bone walls (also seen in Rome). The wide interspaces between the two shells made the structure much lighter and tolerable for the thin walls of the drum and, moreover, had a functional role, enhancing also the stairs leading to the lantern, following the example of the baptistery (for the vertical section see pg. 41).

After such debut Brunelleschi gained many commissions, mostly by corporations and bankers' groups: the **Ospedale degli Innocenti**, the **Sacrestia vecchia** of San Lorenzo, the **Pazzi Chapel**, **San Lorenzo** and **Santo Spirito**.

The inside of the Pazzi Chapel.

For the *Ospedale degli Innocenti*, commissioned by the guild of silk and started in 1419, Brunelleschi used in the façade a completely classical style, which strikes for the harmony of its composition: the rhythm of the structure is obtained by a long portico of round arches, supported by Corinthian columns. This work, defined by some critics the **first classical building** after the end of Ancient Ages, also constitutes a **free interpretation of medieval compositional schemes**: one has to think for example about the use of arches over columns (in classical architecture the columns were connected with a horizontal architrave and the arches were supported by pillars).

In the buildings of the *Sacrestia vecchia* of San Lorenzo (1422-1428) and the *Pazzi Chapel* (1430-1444) Brunelleschi faced the study of **homologue spaces**, trying to proportionally relate them and highlight the **structural hierarchy** inside the building. He also abolished the use of decorative particulars, typical to Gothic art, and underlined the main structure with the use of the *serena* stone that, with its typical greyish colour, makes a great contrast with the plaster, becoming a decoration itself.

The inside of San Lorenzo.

Finally, in the design of the two Florentine churches (*San Lorenzo*, started in 1419, and *Santo Spirito*, designed in 1436 and started in 1444), Brunelleschi demonstrated his **great interest for mathematics**: he developed very complicated proportional modules, which had their basis on the square of the tribune, repeated a fixed number of times to obtain the measure of the central nave, the choir, the transepts, the height of the columns in comparison with the superior part and to their wideness, etc.

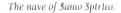

The nave of Santo Spirito.

Brunelleschi's last works became heavier and their composition lost the essentiality that was typical to the style of the architect: this is the case of the *Lanterna del Duomo* and the *Tribune* at the basis of the dome.

Brunelleschi also designed the *Oratorio di Santa Maria degli Angeli*, also called "la Rotonda", which was never finished: it was the first example of an **absolute central plan building** and constituted a very important theoretical example for later generations of architects.

Sculpture

During the XV century sculpture lost its purely decorative role and went on establishing its complete **autonomy and freedom from other arts** as it had been for Greek sculpture. It had a crucial role at renewing the formal language, since sculptors, who often were eclectic artists, synthesised in their works the esthetical ideals of other disciplines.

A sculptor would get his education mostly in **goldsmiths' workshops**, where one would study the drawing and composition of the works and learn various productive methods. Due to the technical progress caused by the workshops and by the examples of master **Ghiberti, the bronze fusion process was spreading out** and its realisation was not assigned to foreigners any more, mostly the Venetians, favoured by the Byzantine tradition, but to **local masters**.

In minor sculpture the genre of the portrait-bust, which was not reliquary any longer, but became a profane monument, synthesis of individualistic humanist values, was becoming popular again together with funeral monuments, very common in the 16th century, which were the union of architecture and sculpture according to Alberti's theory.

Moreover, classical examples were often used to renovate the traditional decorative repertoire, still without totally respecting their symbolic values and often interpreting them with much freedom, in such a way that original proportional laws would not be taken into consideration.

If minor sculpture was a sort of filtered imitation of the ancient, **monumental sculpture was instead a new and original creation**. In this field, in fact, not just a re-discovery of the Greek tradition, only indirectly known through Roman art, but an autonomous artistic development took place

Michelozzo and Donatello, Monumento funerario dell'antipapa Giovanni XXIII (Baldassarre Cossa), commissioned by Cosimo il Vecchio. Note the combination of marble and bronze.

and brought to the renewal of three-dimensional form values.

Renaissance sculpture made, as the other figurative arts, a **synthesis between the interest for truth and the abstraction of forms**, by separating volumes into simple geometrical solids and by studying carefully the chromatic effects of light.

All scientific contemporary knowledge was applied in sculpture: in this way the reliefs were framed by perspective-linear systems and, due to an accurate knowledge of anatomy, the human body, till then forced in static positions, was reconstructed dynamically.

Leaving aside for a while Ghiberti, Donatello and Luca della Robbia – the three greatest sculptors of that time, to whom specific paragraphs will be dedicated – it is now important to remember other crucial artistic characters: Michelozzo, Desiderio da Settignano, Rossellino and Verrocchio.

Desiderio da Settignano, Busto di donna (Florence, Museo Nazionale del Bargello).

MICHELOZZO MICHELOZZI, born in FLORENCE in 1396 and died there in 1472, is famous mostly because of his architectural works, first of all Palazzo Medici-Riccardi and the Medicean villas of Careggi (see pg. 12) and Cafaggiolo (see pg. 13), but was also an important sculptor. Even though few works can be assigned to him alone, since he usually collaborated with other great artists such as Ghiberti and Donatello, these had a great importance for the renovation of Renaissance art. From his sculptures one can feel a sense of **Roman classicism**, re-interpreted through humanistic ideals. As in his architecture, Michelozzo made a **simplification and abstraction of forms**. His reliefs in the **Monumento Aragazzi**, in the cathedral of Montepulciano are famous.

DESIDERIO DA SETTIGNANO, born in SETTIGNANO in 1430 and died in FLORENCE in 1466, pupil of Donatello, interpreted the latter's *stiacciato* (see pg. 58) with great elegance and artistic sensibility. He caused the **diffusion of portrait-busts**, sculptural Roman genre forgotten during the Middle Ages and re-discovered probably by his master. If Donatello, though, in his **Busto di giovane con cammeo** ("Bust of Young Man with Cameo"), only represented an idealised young man, Desiderio came back to the **specific portraying function of the bust**, without neglecting the civil virtues of the portrayed person.

ANTONIO ROSSELLINO, also born in SETTIGNANO (1427), died in FLORENCE (1479), pupil of his brother Bernardo, was a sculptor and an architect close to Alberti's ideas. From Desiderio he took the **delicate treatment of surfaces**. With his brother he created the **type of the Renaissance funeral monument**, which synthesised the schemes of traditional tombs and Roman triumphal arches in a single harmonic structure. In the humanistic tomb, even if the reference to religion was strong, the dead person was glorified mostly for his terrestrial work. One has to mention his **Monumento funerario del cardinale del Portogallo** ("Funeral Monument to the Cardinal of Portugal"; 1461), the **Busto di Matteo Palmieri** ("Matteo Palmieri's Bust"; 1468) and the statue of **San Sebastiano** (1470 approx.).

Andrea di Cione, also called **ANDREA DEL VERROCCHIO**, born in FLORENCE (1435) and died in VENICE (1488), was a sculptor, a painter and a goldsmith. His very personal style, balanced and formally perfect, was full of vigorous three-dimensionality, at the same time softened by a **wise use of *chiaroscuro***. His workshop, the most famous at the times of Lorenzo il Magnifico, was very important because of artists such as Leonardo who worked there. Among his most important works one has to remember his **David** (1475 approx.), the

On the other page, Verrocchio, Dama del mazzolino (Florence, Museo Nazionale del Bargello).

Antonio Rossellino, Monumento funerario del cardinale del Portogallo (Florence, San Miniato).

The doors of the Baptistery

The story of the doors of the Baptistery is very interesting and helps us to understand the cultural environment of the first years of the XV century.

The south door of the Baptistery, as the whole monument, was dedicated to San Giovanni. In the original plan, the north door, facing the countryside, should have been dedicated to the Old Testament and the east door, facing the Cathedral, should have been dedicated to the New Testament, which was considered a more important theme.

In 1401 the contest for the decoration of the two doors was organised. The theme of the contest was Isaac's sacrifice: therefore it seemed obvious that the winner would take care of the Old Testament, meaning the north door. Considering, though, Ghiberti's skills, the commissioners had to face a problem: the time required for such an elaborate artistic creation as the execution of the whole door would probably prevent the same artist from making both of them. For this reason the commissioners thought of starting from the main door, the one dedicated to the New Testament, which, once finished, was placed facing the Cathedral, in the most important position. However, when thirty years later Ghiberti finished the second door, dedicated to the Old Testament, everyone agreed on considering it artistically superior and certainly more modern than the first one. Another problem was then brought up: was it right to limit such a masterpiece, called the *Gate of Paradise*, by putting it in a secondary position or was this door to occupy the more important eastern part, neglecting the theological hierarchy of contents?

Florentine people chose the second option and nowadays one can still admire the *Gate of Paradise* in front of Santa Maria Novella and the *Door of the New Testament* in the northern side of the Baptistery.

Dama del mazzolino (1480 approx.), the ***Incredulità di San Tommaso*** ("St. Thomas' incredulity"; 1476-1483) and the ***Monumento equestre a Bartolomeo Colleoni*** ("Equestrian Monument to Bartolomeo Colleoni") in Venice (1479-1488).

Ghiberti

Sculptor, architect and glass painter, **LORENZO GHIBERTI** (FLORENCE, 1378-1455) started his education in the goldsmith's workshop of Bartoluccio di Michele, who later would become his collaborator and step-father. Ghiberti was a **great master of bronze fusion**, the first one to open a workshop in Florence for bronze workers and founders, where amongst the others Donatello, Paolo Uccello and Michelozzo worked. Ghiberti is considered to be **the connection between late international gothic culture and the Renaissance**, but differently from other great artists of early Renaissance, he never sought for a radical break away from the tradition.

In his first great work, a lobed bronze slab with the scene of the **Sacrificio di Isacco** (Isaac's Sacrifice"; see pg. 46), the style is mainly late gothic, but it already has innovative elements. If on one hand late gothic taste is demonstrated by **a rich compositional layout, detailed realism, great attention to the particulars** and technical precision, on the other hand Renaissance art is foreshadowed by **new naturalism, direct reference to classical sculpture**, attention to **light effects** and **treatment of bronze surface**, an attempt to **develop a sense of depth**.

Due to the success obtained with his first work, Ghiberti had the assignment of the **north door** of the Florentine Baptistery (see pg. 53), following the general scheme of the previous door by Andrea Pisano in which 28 slabs were divided in 7 rows.

The first 20 slabs at the top represent the **Scene della vita e della passione di Cristo** ("Scenes from the Life and Passion of Christ"), the last 8 below represent the **Quattro Evangelisti** ("Four Evangelists") and the **Quattro Dottori della Chiesa** ("Four Wise Men of the Church").

Even though the realisation of this work lasted for long, it shows a **stylistic unity**. However, it is possible to find an **internal evolution**, from **juvenile naturalism** to **mature rationality**. In the same years Ghiberti worked on the cartoons for the windows of the Florentine cathedral, designing the huge compositions of the **Assunzione della Vergine** ("As-

On the other page, the east door of Florentine Baptistery, which Michelangelo defined as The Gate of Heaven.

sumption of the Virgin") for the central eye of the façade (1405) and of **Santo Stefano** and **San Lorenzo** (1413). Between 1432 and 1443 Ghiberti would then work on the cartoons for the windows of the 15 chapels of the tribunes.

In 1415 the artist made the statue of **San Giovanni Battista** ("St. John the Baptist") for the niche of the guild of Calimala in the church of Orsanmichele, which is the **first statue from a single bronze fusion**. Between 1419 and 1422 Ghiberti also worked on the statue of **San Matteo** for the niche of the guild of moneychangers. In 1428 he finally completed the statue of **Santo Stefano** for the niche of the guild of wool, which had already reached a total **three-dimensional autonomy**, in comparison with the previous works. In 1425 Ghiberti started working on the **east door** of the baptistery, which Michelangelo later called the **Porta del Paradiso** ("Gate of Paradise"; see pg. 53), completed only in 1452. The general scheme had to consist of 24 slabs with the **Scene del Vecchio Testamento** ("Scenes of the Old Testament"), which were instead synthesised in **ten big narrative scenes** of rectangular shape, following an organisation of space that had already gone beyond the old gothic model. The work presents a **simultaneous representation of episodes** and the landscape, treated in a completely new way, also with the use of linear perspective, has become the key for interpreting the relations amongst the figures. The *Porta del Paradiso* is probably the first example of **pictorial bas-relief**: it is, in fact, a sculpture in which the relief changes from high to low, in a continuos sequence that creates effects of space and atmospheric width. In this period the artist collaborated with Brunelleschi in the project for the dome of the Florentine cathedral. Ghiberti is also the author of three books called **Commentarii**, in which he wrote about the classical art of Plinio il Vecchio and Vitruvio and modern art, starting from Giotto. In this way Ghiberti favoured the spreading of artistic theories of his time, becoming the **first great modern art historian**.

Donatello

On the other page, San Giorgio (*Florence, Museo Nazionale del Bargello*).

San Giovanni Evangelista, *made by Donatello for a niche at one side of the central door of the cathedral and now kept at the Museo dell'Opera del duomo.*

D onato Niccolò de' Bardi, born in 1386 in a poor family in FLORENCE, where he died in 1466, commonly known as **DONATELLO**, the greatest sculptor of the XV century, did not get any humanistic education, but was dedicated only to the problems and themes of sculpture.

Defined as an **anti-classic** and sometimes **anti-naturalistic** artist, due to the extraordinary power of his creativity and to his incredibly modern talent, Donatello was probably the **most innovative personality** in the forms and in the technique of Renaissance art.

His artistic revolution was definitely not linear. It was a constant going beyond and a progressive enrichment of different stylistic inventions. Due to the heterogeneity of his works, Donatello's art was the starting point for all Renaissance sculptural experimentation, becoming the *exemplum* for many various styles. However, as a result of his incomparable artistic greatness and to his modern spirit, Donatello **remained isolated from the leading art movement**.

After a possible **trip to Rome with Brunelleschi** (the two artists were definitely friends even if artistically divided by clear social differences) in 1404 in order to study classical works, Donatello started his practise in the environment of the artists who worked for the "Fabbrica del Duomo" ("The factory of the cathedral"). At that time the so called "Porta della Mandorla" ("The door of the Almond"), for which Donatello made the left *Profetino* ("Little Prophet") in 1406, was being decorated. It was in this environment where the artist contacted and got influenced by the elder Nanni di Banco (?1390-1421), one of the first artists who started the revival of classical sculpture.

The marble **David**, completed in 1409, the first great work by Donatello, was strongly influenced by late gothic style and by Ghiberti's work (with whom he worked from 1404 till 1407) as far as the absence of facial expressiveness and the stylisation of the hair is concerned. However it already demonstrated signs of originality in the construction of the figure, the dynamic *contrapposto* pose and the treatment of the drapery.

In the **San Marco** – which was made for the niche of the guild of wool in the church of Orsanmichele – and in the seated **San Giovanni Evangelista** ("St. John the Baptist"; 1409-1411) – which was made for a niche on one side of the central entrance to the cathedral – the structure of the works reveals an already deep **knowledge of classical art**, even though many features of gothic idealisation are still present (for instance in the expression of the face). Moreover the technical skills of the young sculptor are obvious and one can already recognise his **innovative power**.

It was only with the **San Giorgio** (1416), made for the niche of the guild of armourers in Orsanmichele, Donatello went beyond the major part of late gothic tradition, completing for the first time a proudly human individual, in a sculptural work that **refused the decorative role, imposed by architectural culture, and found an autonomous space**. In the figure of the saint, which is not solemn at all, the psychological tension comes out from facial mimics and goes perfectly together with the movement of the body. In this work many critics see a classical reference, which is not repetition of models, but resemblance in the portraying process of the character: Donatello **found in the Florentine people the *virtus* that was so much admired in classical culture**.

The **Uccisione del drago** ("Murder of the Dragon"; 1420) for the basis of the niche of San Giorgio, is the first real example of *stiac-*

ciato (pressed) relief: **the thickness of the relief is so limited that one can look at it as a pictorial work**. Deeply engraved lines that create strong effects of shadow, contrasting with the parts of the relief define the masses that are illuminated. The perception of space is obtained by a conscious use of aerial perspective, creating the effect of atmospheric thickness already obtained by Ghiberti.

In the mean time, precisely in 1412, Donatello had already started working on the three-dimensional decoration of Giotto's bell tower, firstly making the statues of the ***Profeta barbuto*** ("Bearded Prophet") and the ***Profeta con cartiglio*** ("Prophet with Cartouche"), in which **facial features are clearly naturalistic**, searching for a pathetic expression. Later on, the sculptor made the strongly dynamic group of the ***Sacrificio di Isacco*** ("Isaac's Sacrifice"; 1421) and the two prophets ***Geremia*** (1426) and ***Abacuc*** (1427). The latter were very **violently realistic** works, particularly the last one, also called the ***Zuccone*** ("Man with a Big Head"), because of the big bold head of the character. The non-rhythmic treatment of the free drapery

Slab with the Banchetto di Erode, *for the font of the Baptistery of Siena.*

reveals in these sculptures the anatomy of the bodies and clearly derives from the juvenile studies of the artist.

In these years the artist also worked on the golden bronze statue of **San Ludovico di Tolosa** (1423) for the shrine of Orsanmichele, later substituted by the group of Verrocchio, in which Donatello demonstrated his ability at treating bronze surfaces, which remain rough in the shadowed parts and very smooth in the illuminated parts.

He also made a bas-relief with the **Madonna Pazzi**, which is interesting for its accurate study of the relations between the mother and the son, and the wooden **Crocifisso** ("Crucifixion") in Santa Croce. The latter was very much criticised by Brunelleschi, who accused Donatello for having "put a farmer on a cross", since the sculptor did not respect the divine proportions that would usually characterise the figure of Christ. However, the anti-naturalistic description of the body (the anatomy is consciously wrong) very strongly expresses human pain.

Between 1425 and 1433 Donatello intensively collaborated with Michelozzo Michelozzi. For the font of the baptistery of Siena he made the innovative slab of the **Banchetto di Erode** ("Feast of Heron"; 1425) that, due to **very rigorous perspective construction** in parallel sections, which shows different scenes of the same episode, demonstrated all the expressive possibilities of Donatello's *stiacciato*. He also made the relief of the **Assunzione** ("Assumption"; 1427) for the sarcophagus in the funeral monument of the cardinal Brancacci di Sant'Angelo a Nilo in Naples. This work, due to its **anti-classic liberty** and **originality of composition**, developed around a vortex of lines slightly engraved in the marble, represents one of the most important works by the artist.

In 1430 Cosimo de' Medici commissioned to Donatello the realisation of the bronze **David** of Bargello, the first example from the ancient times

Choir stalls of the cathedral (Florence, Museo dell'Opera del Duomo).

Detail of the Madonna col Bambino, *made by Donatello for the main altar of the Basilica del Santo in Padova.*

of a **full relief naked figure in natural dimensions**. The young man, portrayed in a tilted hip position, could easily refer to an ancient model: however, the interpretation of the artist is very original and in the shadow of David's hat one can find a touch of melancholy, which expresses not the mythical Olympic peace, but tormented human passion.

All Florentine works before his departure for Padova, in 1443, reveal the new cultural approach of Donatello. In the ***Annuciazione*** ("Annunciation") in Santa Croce (1435) the sculptor framed an enigmatic narration in the classical architraved structure of the shrine, re-interpreted in an anti-classic way and decorated with lively fantasy. The sculptural liberty was also reflected in the ***Choir stalls*** of the cathedral, which were built from 1433 to 1439 (very different from the structure of the contemporary rigorously classic choir stalls of Luca della Robbia and stylistically very similar to the ***Pulpit*** of Prato's cathedral (1433-1438), also by Donatello), in which the **tempestous dance of *putti*** is moving under an artificial double-columned portico. The movement is underlined by the architectural elements, decorated with golden mosaics, which create suggestive light flashes.

Last Florentine works of the period were the two bronze doors for the Sacrestia vecchia di San Lorenzo (1440-1443) with couples of ***Apostoli*** ("Apostles") and ***Martiri*** ("Martyrs"). Even if Brunelleschi did not approve of them because of their clash with the architectural structure, they represent the climax of Donatello's mature art, because of their **dynamic exaltation of the form** and their purely **pictorial development of the sculpture**, completely reduced to the essential.

In PADOVA the artist created two of his greatest masterpieces. The first one is the great altar of the Basilica del Santo (1446-1450), with many reliefs that enhance seven monumental statues, including the **Madonna col bambino** ("Madonna and Child"). The iconography is completely original: the Madonna, in fact, is going to rise from her throne.

Another Donatello's masterpiece in Padova is the equestrian monument of **Gattamelata** (1447-1453), the most classic of his works, paradoxically created in the period in which he was having doubts about the humanistic ideal of the person. These sculptures in a crucial way contributed to the spreading of the Renaissance spirit in the rest of Italy.

Detail of Judith's face, clearly and painfully thoughtful, in opposition to traditional iconography, which would present the heroine of the Bible very determined and even exalted by her role, while cutting Holofernes' head.

After coming back to Florence in 1454, Donatello worked on the group of **Giuditta e Oloferne** ("Judith and Holofernes"), which is not a celebration of the heroic act (Judith, before cutting the head of Holofernes, seems to be thoughtful and strengthless), but a **meditation over the painful consequences of the story**.

In 1460 the bronze **Pulpits** for the church of San Lorenzo, finished by his pupils after his death, the artist's creativity is shown not only by the original architectural structure of sarcophagi supported by four pillars each, but also by the **convulsive rhythm** of the composition and the **play of light**, which exalt and dissolve the figures. Particularly important is the relief of the **Martirio di San Lorenzo** ("St. Lorenz's Martyrdom"), in which the perspective structure and the low point of view invite the observer to **get strongly emotionally involved**.

Painting

In the Renaissance artistic culture painting was considered **the most important art**, the one which corresponded the most with the aesthetic sensitivity of the time. Moreover, painting was the art that expressed in the best way contemporary theoretical knowledge, allowing a greater understanding of reality. Since there were almost no models, painting was barely influenced by classical canons and therefore permitted a greater expressive freedom.

The scientific spirit of the Renaissance was reflected in painting by a **methodical use of *chiaroscuro*** in order to lend three-dimensionality to the drawing and a use of linear **perspective** in order to create "exact" spatial relations. In this way a link amongst painting, sculpture and architecture was established. Differently from other arts, the development of painting, started by Masaccio in Florence, was not gradual: on the contrary, it was a real "explosion".

A painter of that time, in fact, would not search just for a credible representation of reality, but, due to the new theories, he would interpret it and often voluntarily create parallel realities, which had to respect rational values.

Apart from the new theoretical developments of art, in the Renaissance practical innovations were created for painting and particularly for the **fresco technique.** Leonardo's technical experimentation over his own picto-

Paolo Uccello, Monumento equestre a Giovanni Acuto *(Florence, Duomo).*

rial works was famous, even though it did not have great results: the major part of his works soon faded away.

During the whole of the 14th century the *sinopia* (preliminary drawing) **had always been drawn directly on the *arriccio*** (rough plaster), forcing the artist to draw very close to the wall and therefore not allowing him a global vision of his work.

In the 15th century the grid method, probably invented by Domenico Veneziano, **was firstly introduced.** This method allowed a small drawing done on paper to be enlarged and transferred on the wall, still keeping the original proportions. **Later on, the technique of engraving and pouncing big-sized cartoons was introduced:** this method consisted of drawing the figures on paper at the same scale as the ones of the fresco and then piercing the outlines with very thin punches. At this point the artist would just put the cartoon on the fresco area and pounce a bit of graphite along the marked outlines in order to make them appear also on the wall. This process would guarantee greater accuracy of the drawing and a study of particulars.

Domenico Veneziano, Madonna col Bambino, (Florence, Berenson's Collection).

Also for the application of colour Renaissance painters used innovative techniques: often the particulars were completed with **dry colours** and, from the second half of the XV century till the XVI century, **layers of tempera colours were alternated with oil colour layers.** In this way, the tested long lasting effect of tempera colour and the brilliant effect of oil were united. However, the innovation of oil painting would mainly concern painting on wood.

Typical products of XV century art were the polyptyches, big altarpieces consisting of many elements. Starting from late gothic canons, this pictorial genre evolved by introducing frames of Renaissance style: columns, arches and architraves would function as links among various elements and would establish a relation with the surrounding architecture.

Entire paragraphs are going to be dedicated to Masaccio, Beato Angelico and Botticelli. However artists such as Paolo Uccello, Domenico Veneziano, Filippo Lippi and Andrea del Castagno should not be forgotten.

Oil painting

After the first half of the XV century painting on wood changed from tempera colours to oil colours.

Painting with tempera colours had already been the subject of numerous experiments that aimed to obtain naturalistic effects. In fact, if initially the chromatic shading off was obtained by lining up different homogeneously coloured surfaces, at the beginning of the XV century there was a need for a more gradual change from one colour to the other; therefore the shading off effect was reached by overlapping layers of different colours.

This technique had been provided by the introduction of more substantial colours: alternating the use of *tempere magre* (more diluted tempera colour) and *tempere grasse* (more dense tempera colour) provided an effect of atmospheric distance. The evolution which brought to oil painting laid in the *tempere grasse*. In such colours, in fact, the linking effect was no longer guaranteed by traditional substances such as egg yolk, but by resinous ones. The last step was substituting the resinous substances with vegetable oil (linseed or walnut) mixed with turpentine.

Oil colours would guarantee a greater luminosity and a wider range of chromatic tones and, above all, they would dry much slower, in this way allowing an easier application of colour and the possibility of infinite corrections.

This technique, already known in ancient times and widely used by Flemish painters, was introduced in Italy around 1470 by Piero della Francesca and Antonello da Messina. In Florence Verrocchio's workshop, and particularly Leonardo da Vinci, often used this technique.

Paolo di Dono, called **PAOLO UCCEL-LO**, born in the region of CASENTINO, in Prato Vecchio, in 1397 and died in FLORENCE in 1475, knew how to interpret **Masaccio's style** in a personal way, mixing the **geometric simplification of the forms** with the mathematical precision of **perspective** and with **strong chromatic sensitivity**. His most famous works are the *Affreschi della Genesi* ("Frescos of Genesis") in Santa Maria Novella, the windows with the scenes of the *Natività* ("Nativity") and the *Resurrezione* ("Resurrection"), and the *Monumento equestre a Giovanni Acuto* ("Equestrian Monument to Giovanni Acuto"; 1439) in the Florentine cathedral.

DOMENICO VENEZIANO, born as the name indicates in Venice around 1405, was the only foreigner to emerge in the Florentine environment, where he died in 1461. Even if very little of his works remain, Veneziano is considered one of the initiators of Renaissance art.

FILIPPO LIPPI, born in FLORENCE in 1405 and died in SPOLETO in 1469, had an artistic evolution **from Masaccio's three-dimensionality to Angelico's linearity**. Amongst his most important works, different paintings on the theme of the *Madonna col Bambino* ("Madonna with Child"), the *Incoronazione della Vergine* ("Coronation of the Virgin"; 1441-1447), the *Annunciazione* ("Annunciation"), the *Madonna degli Angeli* ("Angels' Madonna") are included.

ANDREA DEL CASTAGNO (SAN GODENZO 1419-FIRENZE 1457) was a pupil of Paolo Uccello. He **synthesised the evidence of Masaccio's forms and the dynamism of Donatello**. In Florence, in the cathedral, he painted the *Monumento equestre a Niccolò da Tolentino* ("Equestrian Monument to Niccolò da Tolentino"; 1456).

Andrea del Castagno, Monumento equestre a Niccolò da Tolentino *(Florence, Duomo).*

On the other page, *Filippo Lippi,* Madonna col Bambino e storie di Sant'Anna *(Florence, Palazzo Pitti).*

Masaccio

Tommaso di ser Giovanni Cassai, called **MASACCIO** (SAN GIOVANNI VALDARNO 1401-ROME 1428), is generally considered the **founder of Renaissance painting**. Even if he died very young, in just over five years of activity he managed to leave amazing effects, which changed contemporary painting. Masaccio's works were so great that even Brunelleschi, after he had heard about his death, said: "we are suffering a great loss". Masaccio remained anonymous till 1422, the year in which he entered the guild of doctors and apothecaries in Florence, where he most probably had already lived for a couple of years with his brother Giovanni. During his whole life, Masaccio was in difficult economical conditions constantly burdened by debt until his death.

After his debut, Masaccio dedicated the major part of his artistic life to the decoration of the Brancacci Chapel, showing complete consciousness of his expressive skills.

This work, commissioned by merchant Felice Brancacci, was started in 1423 by Masolino da Panicale (1383-1440), who did the frescos of the vault and the ones of the lunette, which were later lost. The year after, Masolino was collaborating with Masaccio, who would continue the work that was finished by Filippino Lippi many years later. **Rather than a master-pupil relationship between Masolino and Masaccio, there was an equal association between the two artists, in which two antithetic positions – the old and the new – were confronted**. Masolino was much older than Masaccio and that is also why he was way closer to late gothic tradition. Masaccio saw his masters in Brunelleschi and Donatello, with whom he established intense relations. In fact, it was the older and more expert painter who was influenced by the art of the younger one, within the limits, however, of partial dedication and little consciousness of the Renaissance style.

Within the cycle of frescos, the first work ascribed to Masaccio was the multicoloured landscape of houses in the ***Resurrezione di Tabita*** ("Raising Tabitha"; 1424). In the background he painted a sunlit town square, which,

Masolino and Masaccio, Sant'Anna con la Madonna e il Bambino, work painted around 1425 and kept in the Uffizi.

due to its originality, loses its minor role and becomes the most interesting motif of the painting.

The **Battesimo dei neofiti** ("Baptising the Converts") was the first fresco entirely painted by Masaccio. The innovative features of the painting are the **semicircular perspective construction** – which creates an empty space around the baptised and puts him in an obviously dominating position – and a **careful study of light**. The light is defined by a single light source, which gives unitariness to the painting, and by an energetic use of shadow-light contrast, which underlines the three-dimensionality of the figures that do not any longer depend just on colours.

Masaccio defined the images with few essential brush strokes, eliminated all minor ornamental motives, which were useless for the composition and carefully studied human expression, which was concentrated in the attitudes and the features of the face and was not idealised any more, as in courtly canons, but totally terrestrial: as close as possible to the universal nature of mankind. This work is the first example of the "concise realism" that characterised all the art of the master, who was admired by Vasari for his ability to recreate the things "vive et vere" ("alive and real").

In the **Cacciata di Adamo ed Eva** ("Expulsion of Adam and Eve"), painted on the left pillar of the chapel, the contrast of light is even more violent in order to underline the **drama of the event**.

Since the collaboration for the Brancacci Chapel, it is probable that Masaccio and Masolino had started a workshop together. One of their most important work was the **Sant'Anna con la Madonna e il Bambino** ("St. Ann with Madonna and Child") for the church of Sant'Ambrogio, in which the central figures were painted by Masaccio while the rest of the painting was done by Masolino. In this work the **juxtaposition of the two styles** and **the victory of Masaccio's model** is evident. In the compositional scheme the figure of Sant'Anna should have had the greatest importance (this is witnessed also by the greater size of her halo); Masaccio's Madonna, though, because of her solidity, confines the figure

Detail of the buildings in the background of the Resurrezione di Tabita, *in the Brancacci Chapel, attributed to Masaccio.*

Cacciata dal Paradiso terrestre, *in the Brancacci Chapel.*

of Sant'Anna, which is flat and detached from the central nucleus, in the background.

In 1425 the two masters went to Rome, where the cardinal Branda commissioned to them the frescoes of the church of San Clemente and the **Polittico della neve** ("Polyptych of Snow"), destined to the Colonna Chapel in Santa Maria Maggiore, in which the slab with the **Santi Girolamo e Giovanni Battista** dominates due to its expressive strength. The two works were finished much later, because Masolino left a few months later for HUNGARY and Masaccio decided to go back to Florence in order to continue the decoration of the Brancacci Chapel.

In this period he painted the big fresco of the **Tributo** ("Tribute Money"), one of his masterpieces and one of the first examples of the genre of the **historia figurata** (depicted story). The scene is divided into three different episodes, which are strongly interconnected: a sort of continuos narrative sequence is established by the looks of the characters and their drastic movements, which communicate reciprocally, and by the great natural and architectural landscape. In the dominating central scene of **San Pietro con Cristo e gli Apostoli** ("St. Peter with Christ and the Apostles"), the semicircular position of the apostles exalts the figure of Christ, whose head is also the *focus* of the perspective. **Masaccio reached the climax of his expression in the description of the Apostles**, individually treated in their distinctive features, **and in the description of the bare landscape**, which becomes ideal space, being cleared of any perceptive distraction, still remaining realistic.

The cycle of frescos from the Brancacci chapel was concluded with **San Pietro che risana gli storpi con la sua ombra** ("St. Peter Healing the Sick with His Shadow"), **San Pietro e San Giovanni che distribuiscono i beni alla comunità, mentre Anania rimproverato da Pietro cade fulminato ai piedi del santo** ("St. Peter and St. John Giving Alms and the Death of Ananias") and the **Resurrezione del figlio di Teofilo** ("Raising the Emperor's Son").

In 1426 Masaccio also painted a polyptych, commissioned by Giuliano degli Scarsi for the Chiesa del Carmine, in Pisa, in which the panel of the **Crocifissione** ("Crucifixion") stands out. The figure of Christ, who is tragically conquered by death, explicitly derives from contemporary Donatello's *Crocifisso*.

The last work by Masaccio is the fresco of the **Trinità** ("Trinity"; 1427-1428), in the church of Santa Maria Novella. The scene is surrounded by an **artificial architecture**, inspired by Roman triumphal arches, with a strongly foreshortened vault and a round arch supported by Ionic columns and framed by two high pillars. It most probably is the first example of *quadraturismo*, which is the creation of artificial architectural backgrounds, often related to the real surrounding architecture. The painting is divided into **several spatial levels** in which monumental figures are inserted. These figures, according to the divine hierarchy, rise up and move away form the observer's level, finally reaching their climax in the figure of God. The whole composition follows a **rigorous perspective construction** (that is why some critics think of a probable participation of Brunelleschi in the compositional scheme), which provides a low viewpoint, at the height of the lower margin of the painting. With such a geometrical structure, the figures of Christ and God, situated in very high positions, would result deformed and diminished in comparison with the figures of the commissioners, which are in the foreground and at eye level, even if aligned at the sides of the scene. Masaccio solved the problem by not using different metric scales, as it was popular in all medieval painting (the figures of Saints were bigger than the ones of the commissioners) and decided to transgress perspective rules in order to depict the figures of Christ and God in a totally frontal manner, in a prominent position (see pg. 43). In 1428 Masaccio went back to Rome, together with Masolino, in order to complete the frescos of San Clemente, but there he suddenly died. Even if Masaccio did not have any direct pupils he left some exemplary works, which were the most precious heritage for the following generations of painters. In Masaccio's works those painters recognised the roots of the new attitude towards reality, towards the role of human beings in history, towards the individual, which was and "had to be" expressed in art.

Detail of the fresco of the Tributo in the Brancacci Chapel, where one can see the realistic characterisation of the Apostles.

Beato Angelico

Guido di Pietro Tosini, born in VICCHIO DI MUGELLO around 1400 and died in ROME in 1455. Became a monk named fra' Giovanni da Fiesole and for the **divine nature of his art** is commonly known as **BEATO ANGELICO**.

It is very difficult to date his life precisely. We do not know anything about the date of his birth nor about his first education, which some critics would assign to Lorenzo Monaco (1370-1423). The same chronological problem exists in the field of his artistic works, since his stylistic evolution is apparently incoherent. After an **initial dedication to Masaccio's art**, witnessed by a great sensitivity for his **realism** and **three-dimensionality**, Angelico **returned to more archaic forms**. In order to understand Angelico's art, one has to get into the perspective of a religious man: for the artist **Renaissance innovations**, considered dangerously pagan by the higher ranks of the Dominican Order, which he belonged to, **had to be submitted to religious devotion**, since painting was glorifying God.

The ***Trittico di San Pietro Martire*** ("Triptych of St. Peter, the Martyr") and the altarpiece of the ***Madonna con Bambino e santi*** ("Madonna with Child and Saints") belong to the period between 1420 and 1430. In the latter work Angelico put the **figures in a single frame** (which is an innovative solution for the compositional scheme of the triptych) and converted Masaccio's luminosity into **delicate matching of colour** and a **diffused illumination**, simplifying the forms for an easier understanding.

The ***Imposizione del nome di Battista*** ("Naming the Baptist"), of extreme perspective precision, and the ***Annunciazione*** ("Annunciation") were probably juvenile works.

In the altarpiece of the ***Deposizione*** ("Deposition"), Angelico situated in a pyramid the central group in order to make it fit with the spire

Beato Angelico,
Incoronazione della Vergine
(Paris, Louvre).

gothic frame; he opposed two lateral groups, situated horizontally with a beautiful landscaped background, creating an impression of perfect unity. Vital colours soften the severity of the scene without taking anything away from its solemnity, conveyed by the postures and the realistic expressions of the characters.

The **Incoronazione della Vergine** ("Coronation of the Virgin") was the climax of Angelico's devotion to the Renaissance. In the painting, two rows of kneeling figures, unusually turned with their backs, and a floor-tile strictly foreshortened pavement seem to "absorb" in space the high polychrome stairs with the dominating shrine. The whole composition follows a **great perspective construction**. The joy of the moment is expressed by vital colours and diffused light. The last work strongly influenced by Masaccio was the **Tabernacolo dei Linaioli** ("Tabernacle of the Flax Dressers"), commissioned in 1433, where the facial expressions of the saints on the lateral sides are faithful repetitions of the Carmine Chapel frescos. In 1437 Angelico moved from the monastery of Fiesole to the monastery of San Marco in Florence, in those years renovated by Michelozzo. Here Angelico was assigned to **decorate the walls of the building**, which he completed between 1438 and 1446 with the help of many pupils. Apart from some frescos, clearly related to the previous period, **the whole creation is very homogenous**: the works are formally rigorous and severe colour-wise, of a mythical tone, of a bleak, often pre-Renaissance style. In these frescoes the painter developed a new style, most probably related to that particular environment.

After a short stay in Rome, in 1446 Angelico moved to Orvieto, where he painted the frescos for the San Brizio Chapel in the cathedral. In 1448 he went back to Rome, where the new pope Niccolò V assigned him the decoration of the Niccolina Chapel, with the **Storie dei Santi Stefano e Lorenzo** ("Stories of Saints Stefano and Lorenzo"). In a different cultural background Angelico returned to his innovative art with **greater three dimensional vigour of the figures** and substituted natural landscape with **great architectures, taken from Roman ruins**, which fascinated the painter.

The Virgin in the Annunciazione *of the monastery of San Marco.*

Botticelli

D ue to his interest in humanistic literature and philosophy, Sandro di Mariano Filipepi, called BOTTICELLI, born and died in FLORENCE (1445-1510) was the closest painter to the Medici family circle.

Between 1464 and 1467 Botticelli completed his first practise in the workshop of Filippo Lippi, who passed on to the artist the **ideal of a melancholic feminine beauty**, which was not terrestrial, but **became a contemplation on neo-platonic beauty**, surrounded by a reality out of space and time limits.

Later on, Botticelli was strongly **influenced by Verrocchio's sinuous rhythms and Pollaiolo's use of lines, which he converted from constructive to compositional elements**, harmonic meters of a strongly musical composition, therefore bringing linear Florentine style to its greatest expression. This sensitivity was conveyed since his first works and in the *Fortezza* (1470), still strongly linked to Pollaiolo's three-dimensionality, one can already find the search for a formal harmony based more on matching than on contrasting.

With the *Ritratto di Giuditta* ("Judith's portrait") Botticelli faced the genre of **mythological painting**, where the lyricism still dominates over the subject. The figures have limited expressiveness and are often situated in artificial positions in order to give harmony to the composition. For this reason the painter gave up on Pollaiolo's three-dimensionality and the drapery became an ornamental motif.

The Nascita di Venere, kept in the Uffizi in Florence.

After the *Adorazione dei Magi* ("Adoration of the Magi"; 1475) – celebration of the Medici family, whose members are recognisable in the three Magi and amongst their followers – his friend and patron Lorenzo di Piero de' Medici commissioned to Botticelli the *Allegoria della Primavera* ("Primavera"; 1478), the most famous mythological painting of the 15th century. Various figures, divided into different semantic groups, but combined by a single undulating order, are situated on a background of an orange tree forest and of a lawn blooming with flowers. On the left one sees Mercury and the three dancing Graces, on the right Flora accosted by Zephyr; Venus is the centre and the point of equilibrium of the whole composition.

This work is a **neo-platonic re-interpretation of classical myths** and of an ideal humanistic heaven, surrounded by the harmony of nature. The style, though, is not classical and even goes against the principles of Renaissance art: **the volume is created by the outlines more than by the shadows**.

In 1481-1482 Botticelli was in ROME in order to make three great frescos for the Sistine chapel, with the **Punizione dei ribelli** ("Punishment of the Rebels"), the **Prove di Mosè** ("Trials of Moses") and the **Prove di Cristo** ("Temptations of Christ"): they are beautiful illustrations of isolated episodes, more than real and proper "stories".

After coming back from Rome, Botticelli made the **Nascita di Venere** ("Birth of Venus") for Lorenzo di Piero de' Medici, which is probably an allegory of the creative power of love. The feminine nude, depicted as spiritual quality and physical beauty, was the synthesis of neo-platonic ideals. **The volumes are even more flattened, the shadows almost disappear and the corporal matter is reduced to the minimum**; the line, finally, becomes almost abstract and decorative, as in the waves of the sea.

The last works by Botticelli were strongly influenced by the mystical exaltation produced by the prayers of Savonarola. One can find a sense of **restlessness; the painting becomes darker and the line is broken** with very dramatic effects. The **Calunnia** ("Slander") and the **Crocifissione** ("Crucifixion") – which without consolation interprets the dramatic Florentine historical period after the expulsion of the Medici – are two examples of this artistic period.

Probably the most disturbing figure in the painting of the Calunnia *(Florence, Uffizi).*

Michelangelo

Michelangelo Buonarroti (Caprese 1475-Roma 1564) was the leading character of 16th century art and, according to many critics, the highest representative of Italian art. He was interested in architecture, sculpture, painting and poetry, evolving from a first **classical phase** to a mature **mannerist art**, in many aspects anticipating the **Baroque** even if still using an **original and coherent style**. Michelangelo was solitary and very religious, differently from the leading culture of his time; he was aiming for an **individual expression** and not for a relation with nature; his restless spirit always moved him towards formal perfection, which he thought he had never reached.

Michelangelo started his education in painting in 1488, practising in the workshop of Ghirlandaio. In this environment he did not show any interest for contemporary art nor for the scientific applications that strongly influenced Leonardo; instead he concentrated on re-drawing the paintings of Giotto and Masaccio, which he admired for the monumentality and three-dimensionality of their forms.

The year after he entered the school of sculpture of Bertoldo di Giovanni, where he studied the art of Donatello and Jacopo della Quercia. His talent, demonstrated already in his first works, helped him to obtain Lorenzo il Magnifico's protection. In the Medicean court Michelangelo studied classical art in detail, searching for its spiritual contents. This attitude was influenced by the neo-platonic conceptions of Lorenzo's coterie, which gave him the cultural base for the formation of his own aesthetic ideal: **natural beauty became the reflection of interior beauty**. In the *Maddona della Scala* ("Madonna of the Stairs"), his first famous work, the artist made a **synthesis of Christian tradition and ancient ideals**.

Between 1491 and 1492 Michelangelo made the bas-relief of the *Centauromachia* ("Battle of Centaurs"), whose theme and figurative references (Roman sarcophagi) are classical. This work shows little interest for formal completeness and

Michelangelo, Centauromachia, (Florence, Buonarroti's house).

an **accurate research for three-dimensionality and dynamism**. The Centaurs are depicted in difficult positions, with many torsions foreshortened views and interlacings. The artist already focuses on **naked male figures in movement**, which is the dominating motif of his mature art.

After Lorenzo's death and the beginning of Florentine political crisis, Michelangelo left for VENICE (1494). For a short period he stayed in BOLOGNA, where he made the **Arca di San Domenico** ("Ark of St. Domenico"; 1495), and then came back to Florence, where he was fully involved in Savonarola's religious movement.

Detail of San Matteo, Michelangelo's first non-finished sculpture, kept in the Galleria dell'Accademia.

In 1496 he moved to ROME, where he made the statue of **Bacco** (1496), clearly classical work, and the **Pietà** in the Basilica of San Pietro (1499), which already goes beyond classicism. Few years later, in 1501, he came back to Florence, where he received important assignments for the republic.

The guild of wool commissioned the statues of the **Dodici Apostoli** ("Twelve Apostiles") for the Dome of the cathedral. The artist made only the statue of **San Matteo** (1506) that was left, though, at rough state: it was the **first example of Michelangelo's non-finished works**.

Between 1501 and 1504 Michelangelo worked on the **David** for the Opera del Duomo. This statue, situated in front of Palazzo Vecchio, due to its perfect correspondence between dignity and physical power, is the **symbol of the civil virtues of the Florentine republic**. The biblical character is depicted in classical forms, with the physical idealised beauty. The statue is in static equilibrium, at the same time expressing potential dynamism.

In the **Tondo Pitti** (1503-1505) and in the **Tondo Taddei** (1504), ideologically very distant from the *David*, Michelangelo concentrated on **three-dimensional effects of light**.

Among Michelangelo's first pictorial works one cannot forget the **Tondo Doni** (1503-1504). The composition, clearly sculptural, is complex: in a circular web an **equilibrium of strong dynamic tensions** takes place, in a way that is not typical for the theme of the painting.

In 1504 the master made the cartoon for the fresco of the **Battaglia di Cascina** ("Battle of Cascina") for the sa-

*Michelangelo, Tondo Doni
(Florence, Uffizi).*

lon of Palazzo Vecchio, which commemorated the Florentine victory against Pisa in 1364. This work was an example of Michelangelo's **drawing skill**, which allowed the artist to reproduce anatomically correct bodies in the most difficult positions, with excessive foreshortened views and torsions ever seen before. The equilibrium is guaranteed by the classical pose of ***contrapposto***: a light torsion of the bust in one direction is balanced by a movement of the hips and the legs in the other direction. Due to its innovative power, the cartoon (the real fresco was never done) was defined as the "world's school". It also influenced the young Florentine artists of **Mannerism**.

In 1508 Michelangelo went to ROME in order to decorate the vault of the **Sistine Chapel**, his masterpiece, the **synthesis of previous stylistic researches**, which took four years of hard work. After the admiration for the grandness of his work, Michelangelo would always underline his devotion to sculpture. In a letter to Benedetto Varchi Michelangelo claimed: "The more painting is sculptural and the less sculpture is pictorial, the better".

For the ***Tomba di Giulio II*** ("Tomb of Giulio II"), the project of which went through various events, Michelangelo, between 1513 and 1516, made the statues of **Mosè** ("Moses") and the two **Schiavi** ("Slaves"). After the death of the pope, in 1513, the artist went back to Florence, where he had the assignment of numerous architectural works, thanks to the interest of the new Medicean pope Leone X.

In 1515 Michelangelo won the contest for the ***façade of the church of San Lorenzo***, which he never made because, in 1520, the contract was cancelled and substituted by the assignment of constructing the ***Tombe di Lorenzo e Giuliano de' Medici*** ("Tombs of Lorenzo and Giuliano de' Medici") in the same church. These were situated inside the **Medici Chapel**, designed in 1520 and finished in 1534, symmetrically positioned in respect to Brunelleschi's *Sacrestia*. The square plan clearly derives from Brunelleschi's work, but the three-dimensional volumetric values of architectural elements, with strong projections and recesses, are totally original. In the tombs the figures of the dead are depicted in military clothes, seated on the throne with meditative attitude. Surrounded by sacred architecture, the figures of Day and Night, Dawn and Twilight are situated according to the compositional canons and the typologies of the characters already seen in the Sistine Chapel.

In 1524 the master started the works for the **Biblioteca Laurenziana** ("Laurentian Library"), one of his most original works. A long reading hall with walls rhythmically marked by pillars, anticipated by a monumental entrance, where a very original disposition of architectural elements deny their apparent function (the columns and the architraves are recessed into the wall, with a structural function which would normally belong to the wall).

In 1530, a difficult period for Florence, Michelangelo, named magistrate of the Civil Troops and general supervisor of the fortifications, **designed and constructed various defensive ramparts**.

Between 1530 and 1534 Michelangelo worked for the statues of the **Prigioni**. **Left at rough state, these statues possess the perfection of completed works**. According to Michelangelo the stone already contained the image and the artist's work was limited to the engraiving.

Finally, in 1534, Michelangelo moved for the last time to ROME, where he painted the frescos of the **Giudizio finale** ("Final Judgement"; 1535-1541), work penetrated by religious mysticism, on the altar wall of the Sistine Chapel and the Paolina Chapel (1542-1550).

In 1547 Michelangelo was named the architect of San Pietro and built the enormous **Dome** of the cathedral, organised the town planning of **Piazza del Campidoglio** and designed the **façade of Palazzo Farnese**.

Between 1547 and 1555 Michelangelo worked on the **Pietà** of the Florentine cathedral, work of vital dramatic effects, designed for his funeral monument, remained incomplete and broken by the unsatisfied artist.

The last work of Michelangelo was the **Pietà Rondanini**, to which he dedicated the last days of his life: this work is an important **witness of Michelangelo's creative restlessness**.

The entrance of the Laurentian Library in Florence.

Leonardo

LEONARDO DA VINCI, born in VINCI in 1452 and died in AMBOISE in 1519, was probably the most genial personality of the Renaissance. Full of contradictions, if on one hand he was one of the greatest representatives of the period of the Magnifico, on the other hand because of his solitary character he voluntarily avoided the artistic competition that characterised the Florentine cultural environment. Leonardo loved to call himself "omo sanza lettere" ("man without education") and felt distant from Lorenzo's coterie and from the Platonic Academy, accusing both of having intellectual attitudes and practising abstract philosophical speculation while neglecting empirical scientific research. Leonardo himself was constantly observing, analysing and interpreting the laws of nature, looking for their possible practical applications. The artist studied anatomy and mechanics and worked in the fields of optics, astronomy, chemistry and geology. His projects often involved the inventions of modern technology: one should think about flying machinery, nautical instruments (such as the submarine) and war machinery.

Leonardo registered the results of his studies in numerous manuals of notes and technical drawings, among which one has to remember the famous ***Codice atlantico*** ("Atlantic Manuscript"), published for the first time in 1888. In his often fragmentary writings one can feel the **almost mythical enthusiasm** of a man who is looking for the divine in his studies of nature.

In the artistic field Leonardo was mostly dedicated to painting, which he considered the art "of greatest mental challenge", the art, in which the effort was more intense in the theoretical field than the mechanical one. Follower of Florentine naturalism, Leonardo studied new methods to graphically and pictorially visualise natural phenomena and often sacrificed his artistic creations to science, using them for technical experimentation, which was often harmful to this creations.

In1469 Leonardo entered Verrocchio's workshop, the most famous Florentine workshop of that

Leonardo, Ritratto di Ginevra Benci *(London, National Gallery of Art).*

time, and there started his **studies on anatomy and perspective**. From Verrocchio he inherited great **compositional skills** and a great sense of **equilibrium** and **formal order**. In drawing he soon demonstrated a certain independence: he concentrated on the attitudes and natural expressions of the figures and used a softened *chiaroscuro*, in order to make the outlines fade and create an atmospheric illusion, reinforced by the studies on aerial perspective. In this way **he created the "*sfumato*" (fading) technique**.

Annunciazione (*Florence, Uffizi*).

One of Leonardo's first works was the **Ritratto di Ginevra Benci** ("Portrait of Ginevra Benci"), painted in 1474. The painting, whose lower part was later cut off, originally had a very innovative composition with the whole bust of the female figure depicted from a diagonal point of view. For the first time also the hands were represented: the same scheme would be later used by Verrocchio for his *Dama del mazzolino*. The interesting natural background has a **series of light levels**: from the splendour of the face to the darkness of the bush that frames it, to the luminosity of the landscape.

In the **Battesimo di Cristo** ("Baptisim of Christ"; 1475-1478), painted in collaboration with Verrocchio and probably also with Botticelli, the figure of the left angel emerges: the harmony of the shape and the vitality of the face represent the **synthesis of physical description and the expression of a state of mind**.

Leonardo started going beyond Verrocchio's art with the **Annunciazione** ("Annunciation"), painted between 1475 and 1478. The composition and the typology of the characters are traditional and the treatment of the drapery seems to be a simple demonstration of technical skills. One can find, though, the signs of his mature art in the **naturalistic attention for the landscape**, which is near Flemish art. Leonardo did not use defined outlines, which were typical of Florentine drawing, and studied **all possible passages between light and shadows**. The outlines of human figures are softened by a delicate *chiaroscuro*

Adorazione dei Magi
(Florence, Uffizi).

and, in the distance, one can see a progression of alternating light and dark planes.

In 1480 Leonardo painted his **San Girolamo**, following the canons of a long iconographic tradition. This work, interrupted at a preliminary stage, gives us the opportunity of studying the brown preparation of the painting and of evaluating, through its difficult foreshortened view the accuracy of Leonardo's anatomical studies and his knowledge of proportional laws.

The last work of this period was the **Adorazione dei Magi** ("Adoration of the Magi"), commissioned by the monks of the convent of San Donato a Scopeto in 1481 and never finished because of Leonardo's departure for MILAN. The **drawing** with **fast and deep marks** and the perfectly measured *chiaroscuro* with light touches of white lead, which point out the **light effects** and enforce the contrast between the figures in the foreground and the elements in the background, give vitality and movement to this composition. A vortex of human figures rotates around the group of the Madonna and Child, which is the nucleus and the light source of the whole scene.

In 1482 Lorenzo il Magnifico sent Leonardo as a great musician to MILAN to donate a cither to Ludovico il Moro. In the new court the artist found a more suitable environment for his nature and decided to stay there till 1499. In these years Leonardo studied military strategy, was interested in architecture, produced the big model of the **Statua equestre di Francesco Sforza** ("Equestrian Statue to Francesco Sforza"), destroyed by the French in 1499. In the same period Leonardo painted two of his greatest works: the **Vergine delle Rocce** ("Virgin of the Rocks") and the **Ultima cena** ("Last supper"; 1495-1497) in the monastery of Santa Maria delle Grazie.

In 1499, while the French troops were getting closer, Ludovico il Moro fled from Milan and Leonardo began a series of trips, which brought him to MANTOVA, VENICE, FLORENCE (in 1501) and to ROMAGNA as the military engineer of Cesare Borgia's troops. In 1502 he finally came back to FLORENCE. Here Leonardo was assigned to paint the fresco of the **Battaglia di Anghiari** ("Battle of Anghiari"; episode of the war between Florence and the Visconti) in the salon of Palazzo Vecchio, competing in this way with Michelangelo who made the fresco of the *Battaglia di Cascina* on the opposite wall. Also in the latter work Leonardo used innovative techniques, which made the painting disappear in few years.

Around 1503 he started the world wide famous portrait of Monna Lisa di Giocondo, known with the name of **La Gioconda**, which he finished many years later. The portrait represents the bust of a lady diagonally tilted and follows the compositional canons already experimented in the *Ritratto di Ginevra Benci*, and is surrounded by an imaginary rocky landscape, made even more suggestive by the **twilight**.

The atmospheric fluidity of the landscape, present in the treatment of the scarf and the hair, penetrates the figure of the noble woman and contributes to the expression of melancholy-anxiety.

In 1506 Leonardo moved again to MILAN, where he worked for the French ruler, studying hydraulic engineering in order to regulate the river Adda and fortify the Naviglio canal at San Cristoforo. In these years the artist **was constantly in contact with the Florentine environment**. and more than once went to the Medicean city. He also made his last pictorial works: the group of the **Sant'Anna con Madonna e Bambino** ("St. Ann with Madonna and Child"), whose cartoon was already done in Florence in 1501, and the **San Giovanni Battista** ("St. John the Baptist"; 1508-1513).

In 1512 Leonardo left Milan for ROME where he stayed till 1516, under the protection of Giuliano de' Medici, a nephew of pope Leone X. Here he was in contact with the two greatest artistic personalities of that time: Michelangelo and Raffaello, but had to face the competitive environment that bothered the artist in Florence. For this reason, in 1516, when Giuliano de' Medici died, he accepted the invitation of the king of France and moved to his court. Here Leonardo spent the last years of his life passionately studying and completing his previous works.

La Gioconda *(Paris, Louvre)*.

Craftsmen or artists?

The education of Renaissance artists usually took place in the goldsmiths' workshops. What nowadays would be called "fine crafts", during the Middle Ages was the main art. In the 15th century, gold handicraft still had a tradition of technical knowledge that was crucial for the artists who wanted an eclectic education, following contemporary culture. Moreover, the workshops, often hosting foreign artists, became places where to meet and compare different experiences.

In the goldsmiths' environment the artist faced the difficulties of drawing and the technical problems, derived from different materials and working processes. After Humanism had indicated the qualifying moment of artistic production in the theorising process and not in the material work any longer, the **design** had become crucial in any field. Therefore an artist would learn the new approach to his work through the practise of drawing.

Such intellectual conceptions did not diminish the value of the **practical innovations** introduced by handicraft. **The workshops were a sort of scientific laborato-**

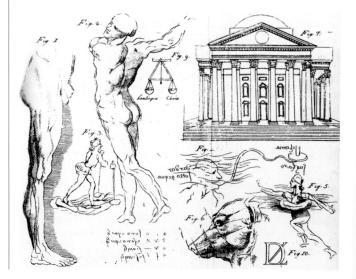

The reproduced picture, from the Trattato della pittura *by Leonardo da Vinci, gives us an idea of the creative procedure of this extraordinary craftsman-artist-scientist.*

ry, and the experiments carried out, influenced all the different fields of social life. Leonardo became passionate for mechanical arts during his experience in the workshop of Verrocchio.

On the other hand, modern engineering finds its origins in applied arts, typical of Renaissance handicraft. Art, science and handicrafts were, in their distinct characteristics, three inseparable fields, because they were dependant on each other. Sometimes art would stimulate the scientific-technologic development: let us think of the knowledge of metals and the fusion process due to the spreading of bronze sculpture. Other times art would use scientific knowledge already acquired in other fields for its own purposes: let us think of medicine and anatomy.

Florentine craftsmen were famous in the whole of Europe for their technical skills. The contemporary leadership of **Tuscan *terracotta*** has its origins in the Renaissance production of ceramics: one should not forget about the famous **majolica of Cafaggiolo**, whose production was supported by Lorenzo il Magnifico.

The already mentioned metallurgic development brought a great production of weapons and the re-discovery of classical **commemorative medals**.

Florence also emerged in the **silk production**. the city had the advantage of advanced machinery and highly specialised craftsmen.

Precious silk embroidery on velvet (1480).

Not always, though, the typical Florentine search for formal perfection produced positive social-economical effects. For centuries, in fact, Florence had been among the best European producers of woollen cloth. In the 16th century the city kept an organisation of work controlled by guilds. This resulted in the production of excellent cloth, but due to the Florentine economical crisis their market was gradually becoming more elitist and limited: for this reason the prices stayed very high and the necessary productive innovations did not take place as they did, instead, in other parts of Europe.

Della Robbia's *Terrecotte*

The **DELLA ROBBIA** family, already famous for its sculptors in the 14th century, became a main character of Florentine art because of **LUCA** (FLORENCE 1400-1482), who started the production of glazed *terrecotte* (baked clay). Even if this procedure was already known at that period, Luca was the first who used it in sculpture, giving it a role, which went far beyond the simple decorative effect.

After a probable education as goldsmith, Luca started to work with marble, leaving some really important works, such as the ***Choir stalls***, which were commissioned to him in 1431 for the Florentine cathedral, and now kept in the Museum of the Opera del Duomo. The Choir stalls by Luca, organised following soft and fluid volumetric passages of *chiaroscuro*, convey his attention to ***classical purity*** and, being very moderated, clearly differ from Donatello's choir stalls, which are pervaded by strong dynamics. Around 1437-1439 the artist made five slabs for the bell tower of the cathedral with the ***Arti liberali*** ("Liberal Arts"), influenced by gothic taste.

Luca della Robbia, Cantori, detail from the relief of the Choir stalls (Florence, Museo dell'Opera del Duomo).

Later on Luca dedicated himself to various architectural and sculptural groups, where, on the **marble structure**, in order to underline the frieze and the ornate, he used for the first time **a cover of coloured terracotta**. The most important work of this period is the ***Ciborium***, completed in 1441 for the church of Santa Maria Nuova and now kept in the church of Santa Maria in Peretola.

Differently from his followers, Luca used few colours: light blue for the background, white for the figures, yellow and green for the festoons and few other colours for the splendid friezes with fruit and flowers which, with their richness, would contribute to the luminous freshness of the figures.

Luca created numerous works at his mature stage: particular attention should be given to the **tondi** with the **Apostoli** ("Apostles") in the Pazzi Chapel, the lunettes with the **Ressurezione** ("Resurrection"; 1442-1445) and the **Ascensione** ("Ascension"; 1446-1451) in the cathedral, to the **Tomba del vescovo Federighi** ("The Tomb of Bishop Federighi") in Santissima Trinità, the **Ceiling** of the Cardinal of Portugal Chapel in San Miniato al Monte (1461-1466).

A theme dear to the artist was the groups of the **Madonne col bambino** ("Madonna with child"), made in full or bass-relief inside the lunettes (among which the **lunette in via dell'Agnolo**, the **Madonna del roseto** ("Madonna of the Roses") and the **Madonna della mela** ("Madonna of the Apple") all kept in the museum of Bargello) where the purity of the images and the essentiality of the compositional scheme unite with the expressiveness of the faces.

Luca della Robbia, Madonna del roseto (Florence, Museo Nazionale del Bargello).

During the last years of his life Luca collaborated with his nephew **ANDREA** (1435-1525) who in his juvenile works was so close to his predecessor that it caused much confusion at indicating the author of the works. Later on he was influenced by many contemporary artists, first of them Verrocchio; and developed a sensitivity more distant from Luca's essentialism and more related to **crowded contemporary schemes**. Valuable works of his are the **Putti entro tondi**, which decorate the portico of Innocenti, and the **Incontro di San Domenico e di Francesco** ("St. Domenico meeting St. Francesco") in the portico of San Paolo.

The tradition of Della Robbia was followed by a son of Andrea, **GIOVANNI** (1469-1529), who, together with Santi Buglioni, contributed to the spreading of glazed terracotta all over Tuscany.

Cellini's gold

B ENVENUTO CELLINI (FLORENCE, 1500-1571) as most of the artists of the Renaissance was an eclectic: firstly a goldsmith, then a sculptor and, in the end, a writer. However, the activity which made him so famous was that of goldsmith, to which he was devoted already very young, after an unsuccessful attempt to follow a musical education. In 1523 he moved to ROME and his fame was so wide, that Cellini got the protection of pope Clemente VII, who, in 1529 named **him** the **master of the papal mint**. For the pope and Roman cardinals Cellini made numerous goldsmith's objects (medals, jewellery, china etc.) which unfortunately were lost.

In these years his artistic activity was followed by episodes of fights and violence, which caused Cellini's imprisonment. Called to France by king Francesco I, in 1543 Cellini made him the famous golden enamel *Saltcellar*, initially destined to cardinal Ippolito d'Este. The composition consists of Neptune and Earth one in front of the other, surrounded by a big group of Nereids, Nymphs and animals. The influence of the Florentine school can be seen in the monumental scheme of the work, which is considered sculpture in miniature.

During the same period Cellini started to be interested in monumental sculpture, using his experience, gained in Rome and from the lessons of

Benvenuto Cellini, Cosimo I (Florence, Museo Nazionale del Bargello).

Michelangelo and Raffael-lo. Nowadays his **Ninfa di Fontainbleau** is admired by the French for its sophisti-cated mannerism.

In 1545 Cellini came back to FLORENCE where he was welcomed by Cosimo I, who commis-sioned to the artist the bronze portrait-bust of **Perseo**. After his death in 1571, two big marble statues were found in his studio: the **Apollo e Giac-into** and the **Narciso**, interesting for the interpretation of Cellini's artistic evolution.

Benvenuto Cellini, Saltcellar in gold and enamel (Vienna, Kunsthistorisches Museum).

The works of the master were considered unreachable be-cause of their **technical and expressive characteristics** and his **sophistication** although the details would often disturb the equilibrium of the unity: that is where the limit of Cellini as a sculptor lay. However, the artist sug-gested to mannerist Florentine sculpture many innova-tions, first of all the **dynamics** of his free figures, which allowed various viewpoints.

In two **Treatises**, which he wrote about goldsmith's art and sculpture, **art is considered divine**, a sort of reli-gious ritual where he has the role of a priest. From an artistic point of view, instead, the absolutely pragmatic at-titude of Cellini, who concentrates much more on techni-cal than on creative aspects, dominates.

As far as Cellini as a writer is concerned, one has to re-member his **Vita** ("Life"), one of the most vital examples of Italian literature of the 16th century, which was very much appreciated during the Romanticism period be-cause of the **exaltation of individualism**, which is the main theme of the work.

Florence for the world

Piero della Francesca, Ritratto di Federico da Montefeltro.

T he Uffizi gallery, founded by the Medici family in Florence on the ruins of the old Romanesque church of San Pietro Scheraggio (which are still recognisable on the first floor) in 1581, is the most important art gallery in Italy and one of the most ancient and prestigious galleries in the world. The museum contains about five hundred Italian and foreign works between XIII and XVIII centuries with the largest collection of Renaissance paintings of the world.

Such a collection does not allow a more detailed analysis of single works which would deserve more attention; however it is possible to indicate stylistic and thematic paths, leaving aside the individual styles of the authors. However, the greatest Renaissance works have already been taken into consideration in the previous pages.

The collection of Tuscan paintings from the 13th and the 14th century contains the **Madonna in maestà** ("Majestic Madonna") by Cimabue (1240-1302), the **Madonna in trono col Bambino** ("Madonna in the Throne") by **DUCCIO DI BUONINSEGNA** (1255 approx.-1318), the **Madonna col Bambino** ("Madonna with Child"), **Angeli e Santi** ("Angels and Saints") e il **Polittico di Badia** ("Polyptych of Badia") by **GIOTTO** (1267 approx.-1337).

The 14th century is represented in particular by painters from Florence and Siena: **GIOTTINO**, **SIMONE MARTINI** (1284 approx.-1344; **Annunciazione**, "Annunciation"), **PIETRO** e **AMBROGIO LORENZETTI**.

The halls reserved to the Tuscany 15th century help to understand the evolution from international Gothic, in the first years of the century – with paintings by **LORENZO MONACO** and **GENTILE DA FABRIANO** – to early Renaissance.

Amongst the most representative works one finds the **Battaglia di San Romano** ("Battle of San Romano") by **PAOLO UCCELLO** (1397-1475), the group of the **Madonna e Sant'Anna** by **MASACCIO** (1401-1428) and **MASOLINO** (1383-1440), the **Madonna e Santi** by **DOMENICO VENEZIANO**

a. *Giovanni Bellini,* Allegoria sacra.

b. *Raffaello,* Ritratto di Giulio II.

c. *Rosso Fiorentino,* Madonna e santi.

d. *Parmigianino,* Madonna dal collo lungo.

a

b

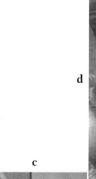

d

c

Tiziano, Venere di Urbino.

(1405-1461), the **Incoronazione della Vergine** ("Coronation of the Virgin") by **BEATO ANGELICO** (1400 approx.-1455), the **Ritratti di Federico da Montefeltro e di Battista Sforza** ("Portraits of Federico da Montefeltro and of Battista Sforza") by **PIERO DELLA FRANCESCA** (1420 approx.-1492), the **Battesimo di Cristo** ("Baptisim of Christ") by VERROCCHIO (1435-1488), the **Adorazione dei Magi** ("Adoration of the Magi") and the **Annunciazione** ("Annunciation") by **LEONARDO DA VINCI** (1452-1519).

There are many paintings by **FILIPPO** (1405-1469) and **FILIPPINO LIPPI** (1457-1504), **ALESSIO BALDOVINETTI** (1425-1499), **ANTONIO POLLAIOLO** (1431-1498), **ANDREA MANTEGNA** (1431-1506), **DOMENICO GHIRLANDAIO** (1449-1494) and **HUGO VAN DER GOES** (1440 approx.-1482).

However, the most brilliant collection is **BOTTICELLI**'s (1445-1510). It contains almost all the greatest works of the master, such as the **Fortezza**, the **Adorazione dei Magi** ("Adoration of the Magi"), the **Allegoria della Primavera** ("Primavera"), the **Nascita di Venere** ("Birth of Venus"), the **Madonna del Magnificat** ("Magnificat Madonna") and the **Calunnia** ("Slander").

The 14th century is concluded by **Venetian painting**, in particular the **Allegoria sacra** ("Sacred Allegory") by **GIOVANNI BELLINI** (1430-1516), **Mosè e il Faraone** ("Moses and the Pharaoh") by **GIORGIONE** (1478-1510) and some paintings by **CARPACCIO**. It also contains a representative group of **German and Flemish masters**: one should note the **Portrait of the Father** and the **Adoration of the Magi** by **ALBRECHT DÜRER** (1471-1528); the works of **CRANACH**, **H. HOLBEIN**, **ALTDORFER**.

The paintings of the 16th century in Tuscany include some paintings by **PONTORMO** and by **PERUGINO**, various works by **ANDREA DEL SARTO**, **LUCA SIGNORELLI** and **ROSSO FIORENTINO** and some examples of Mannerism by **BRONZINO** and **ALESSANDRO ALLORI**.

In the XVI century **PARMIGIANINO** and the **Emilians**,

were active together with the current of Mannerism of **CARRACCI**, the **Lombardians CORREGGIO** e **BERNARDINO LUINI**, the **Venetians LORENZO LOTTO** (**Ritratto di giovane** ("Portrait of a young man"), **VERONESE**, **TINTORETTO**, **SEBASTIANO DEL PIOMBO** and **DOSSO DOSSI**.

The path through the great Italian paintings of the 15th and the 16th century is very interesting: from **RAFFAELLO** (**San Giovannino**, Madonna **del cardellino** ("Madonna of the Goldfinch"), the portraits of **Giulio II**, **Leone X** and **Francesco Maria della Rovere**), to the **Sacra Famiglia** by **MICHELANGELO**, from **TIZIANO** (**Flora**, **Venere di Urbino** ("Urbino Venus"), **Venere e Cupido** ("Venus and Cupid"), **Ritratto di un Cavaliere di Malta** ("Portrait of a Knight of Malta"), **Ritratto di Francesco Maria della Rovere** ("Portrait of Francesco Maria della Rovere"), to **CARAVAGGIO** (with the **Bacco adolescente** ("Adolescent Bacchus"), the **Sacrificio di Isacco** ("Isaac's sacrifice") and the **Medusa**).

Another interesting collection of works is from the **North Europeans Artists of the 17th century**, which contains the paintings by **RUBENS** (1577-1640), portraits by VAN DYCK (1599-1641), the **Old Rabbi** and **Self-portraits** by **REMBRANDT** (1606-1669).

The 18th century is mostly represented by the **Venetian** works of **CANALETTO** and **FRANCESCO GUARDI**.

Caravaggio, Bacco

Apart from pictorial works, the Uffizi contain some important **Florentine and Flemish tapestries** and famous examples of **classical sculpture**: the **Ermafrodito** ("Hermaphrodite") from the II century B.C., the famous **Venere dei Medici** ("Medici Venus"; copy from the I century B.C. of an original inspired by **PRASSITELE**), the statues of **Niobe e i suoi figli saettati da Apollo e da Diana** ("Apollo and Diana Shooting Niobe and her children"; copies of SCOPA's works) and various Roman busts and statues.

In 1993 a bomb, most probably an attempt by the Mafia, exploded near the Uffizi. This caused serious damage to the structure of the building and to some works of the collection.

Essential bibliography

G.C. ARGAN, *Storia dell'arte italiana*, Sansoni Editore, Florence 1968

E. BAIRATI - A. FINOCCHI, *Arte in Italia*, Loescher Editore, Turin 1984

P. BARGELLINI, *La splendida storia di Firenze*, Vallecchi Editore, Florence 1964

B. BERENSON, *I pittori italiani del Rinascimento*, Hoepli, Milan 1936

C. BERTELLI - G. BRIGANTI - A. GIULIANO, *Storia dell'arte italiana*, Edizioni Electa/Bruno Mondadori, Milan 1986

P.P. BOBER - R.O. RUSTEIN, *Renaissance Artists and Antique Sculpture*, London 1991

J. BURCKHARDT, *La civiltà del Rinascimento in Italia*, Sansoni Editore, Florence 1940

C. CENNINI, *Trattato della pittura*, Longanesi, Milan 1975

F. DE SANCTIS, *Storia della letteratura italiana*, Rizzoli, Milan 1983

E. GARIN, *La cultura filosofica del Rinascimento italiano*, Sansoni Editore, Florence 1961

E. GARIN, *Medioevo e Rinascimento*, Laterza, Bari 1961

H. GRIMM, *Michelangelo*, Dall'Oglio, Milan 1964

D. HAY, *Profilo storico del Rinascimento italiano*, Biblioteca Sansoni, Florence, 1966

J.R. HALE, *Firenze e i Medici*, Mursia, Milan 1980

L.H. HEYDENREICH, *Il primo Rinascimento*, Rizzoli Editore, Milan 1974

J. LUCAS - DUBRETON, *La vita quotidiana a Firenze ai tempi dei Medici*, Biblioteca Universale Rizzoli, Milan 1985

P.C. MARANI, *Leonardo*, Electa, Milan 1994

F. NEGRI ARNOLDI, *Storia dell'arte*, Gruppo Editoriale Fabbri, Milan 1984

A. PANELLA, *Storia di Firenze*, Sansoni, Florence 1949

V. ROSSI, *Storia della letteratura italiana*, Vallardi, Milan 1946

I.B. SUPINO, *Sandro Botticelli*, Formiggini, Modena 1909

P. VILLARI, *Niccolò Machiavelli e i suoi tempi*, Hoepli, Milan 1895

R. VILLARI, *Storia medioevale*, Editori Laterza, Bari 1978

R. VILLARI, *Storia moderna*, Editori Laterza, Bari 1978

G. VOIGT, *Il risorgimento dell'antichità classica*, Sansoni, Florence 1968

Contents

Finito di stampare nel mese di aprile 2001
dalle Grafiche BUSTI S.r.l.
Colognola ai Colli (Verona)